Managing and Analyzing Your Collection

A Practical Guide for Small Libraries and School Media Centers

Carol A. Doll
Pamela Petrick Barron

American Library Association
Chicago and London
2002

While extensive effort has gone into ensuring the reliability of information appearing in this book, the publisher makes no warranty, express or implied, on the accuracy or reliability of the information, and does not assume and hereby disclaims any liability to any person for any loss or damage caused by errors or omissions in this publication.

Composition by the dotted i in Melior and Univers Condensed using QuarkXpress 4.1 for the Macintosh

Printed on 60-pound white offset, a pH-neutral stock, and bound in 10-point cover stock by Batson Printing

The paper used in this publication meets the minimum requirements of American National Standard for Information Sciences—Permanence of Paper for Printed Library Materials, ANSI Z39.48-1992. ♾

Library of Congress Cataloging-in-Publication Data

Doll, Carol Ann, 1949–
Managing and analyzing your collection : a practical guide for small libraries and school media centers / by Carol A. Doll and Pamela Petrick Barron.
p. cm.
Includes bibliographical references.
ISBN 0-8389-0821-7
1. Collection management (Libraries)—United States—Statistical methods. 2. Small libraries—Collection development—United States—Statistical methods. 3. School libraries—Collection development—United States—Statistical methods. I. Barron, Pamela Petrick. II. Title.
Z687.2.U6 D65 2002
025.2′1′0973—dc21 2001053747

Printed in the United States of America.

06 05 04 03 02 5 4 3 2 1

CONTENTS

INTRODUCTION

The purpose of this book is to introduce you to a simple technique that you can use to evaluate your library collection. By using this technique to gather statistical information about your collection, you will be able to make more informed decisions regarding the development of that collection. By using the data generated from this technique, librarians have been able to obtain additional funding for their libraries. Being able to acquire additional funding for collection development is an important consideration in these days of rising costs, shrinking budgets, and increasing technological demands.

Librarians throughout the United States have used this technique successfully for more than fifteen years. The authors began by working with media specialists in South Carolina and taught them how to use this technique. School library media specialists in a Florence, South Carolina, school district were able to get a bond referendum for library resources passed. Charleston, South Carolina, media specialists conducted a district-wide analysis that convinced school administrators to allocate additional funding for library resources. After presenting a workshop to a group of school media specialists on the South Carolina coast, a school district administrator told the authors that he could endorse their techniques because it gave him some solid evidence for making decisions about allocating funds to media centers. Since then, the technique has been adapted for use in a wide variety of library settings across the

United States. The authors regularly teach students how to use this technique. Changes made since the publication of *Collection Analysis for the School Library Media Center* (ALA, 1991) are reflected in this work. We are convinced the techniques described here are still valid and useful.

By using these techniques, prospective and practicing librarians have learned to apply research techniques effectively. In the places where this technique has been utilized, there is also a clearer understanding of the state of library collections based on real data rather than subjective impressions.

In this volume we present our ideas using a cookbook approach. We provide the recipe; you supply your own ingredients. Do not be dismayed to discover spread sheets, mathematical calculations, and statistics. You *can* do it! Just take one step at a time. Follow the directions or fill in the blanks on the form and before you know it, you will have gathered some valid data that you can use to your advantage.

We would like to hear from you. Please let us know what you accomplish.

Good luck!

Pamela Petrick Barron
Carol A. Doll

ONE

Management Objectives

What Is a Collection Analysis?

As librarians, we are well aware of the wide range of services we make available to our patrons. Central to these services is the development of a collection of resources to meet the needs of the users. Library collections are created in order to be used. How are *useful* and *relevant* library collections created? It does not happen by accident. There has to be a systematic process in place to follow, and this process has come to be called collection development. The Washington Library Media Association has an excellent definition:

> Collection development is most effective when guided by a plan of action which is periodically reviewed to ensure that the plan is adequate to develop a collection which reflects current needs of students and teachers. Factors to include in the plan are:
>
> - Philosophy and goals of the school and library media program
> - Projected size of the collection
> - Systematic review of each category of materials
> - Renewal rates for different categories of material in the collection
> - Identification of areas of specialization to meet curricular emphasis and unusual needs
> - Criteria for selection of materials

- Criteria to identify materials to be replaced or discarded
- Process to identify user needs and their involvement with selection
- Characteristics of users to be served
- Priorities for acquisition
- Identification of funding sources
- Compilation of a future acquisitions list.[1]

According to G. Edward Evans, there are six definable elements in collection development: (1) community analysis, (2) policies, (3) selection, (4) acquisition, (5) weeding, and (6) evaluation.[2] Thus, collection evaluation or analysis is just one aspect of collection development, and it is the focus of this book.

The purpose of a collection analysis is to determine the quality of the collection. Quality may be measured in numerous ways. Underlying the notion of quality is *management,* the effective combination of resources to achieve a desired outcome. *Information Power: Building Partnerships for Learning* supports this concept:

> Efficient and creative management is key to maintaining a student-centered library media program. Strong management skills are required to orchestrate a wide variety of complex technologies and resources and to supervise the specialized staff required to support them. A well-managed program organizes people, funds, equipment, time and a full range of physical resources and provides the highest level of service to students, teachers, administrators, community members, and others.[3]

The vocabulary of management principles includes the following terms: *systematic, measurable, efficient, effective, input, output, inner environment,* and *outer environment.* Almost all of the systematic management techniques or methods contain these elements: the systematic allocation of resources; an evaluation of their effectiveness; and the ability to communicate both need and effectiveness of resource allocation to all of those involved in the process.

Evaluation of a library collection usually falls into two categories: (1) the evaluation of the collection itself, usually in terms of numbers, quality, currency, or similar measures, and (perhaps most important) (2) how well the collection serves the needs of the users. Because meeting the needs of the library's users is so important, any collection analysis should include a needs assessment, that is, an analysis of the community that the library serves, including current and future users. We need to know where we are before we can know where we are going.

We also need to consider how we will define the term *collection.* Today, because of technology, we have access to a great deal of information beyond the four walls of a library. So how we define the collection will influence the selection of our resources. To think of your collection only within the physical boundaries of your library will create a limited view of the collection. You need to consider availability and accessibility when defining your collections. If a resource is available, that simply means it exists and can be located. For a resource to be accessible, it must be physically present.[4] The time interval between accessible and available can be critical for our users.

Once we have a working definition of a collection, determining the quality of it can be difficult partly because of the various ways that collections have been measured. For example, references to recommended collection size can be misleading, for size alone does not guarantee that the appropriate items will be included. In the past, often quantifiable rather than qualitative measures were used to evaluate library collections, most particularly those in schools. The first edition of *Information Power: Guidelines for School Library Media Programs* addressed this:

> Adequacy of the collection size is best determined through an evaluation of how well the collection and information services are meeting the needs of the users. Criteria that can be applied to assess the adequacy of collection size include determining whether the collection is large enough to satisfy a certain percentage of requests, whether it represents basic titles and sources recommended in standard selection tools, and whether, as judged by users themselves, it offers sufficient materials to stimulate and promote literacy development and to support special program

emphases. An overriding concern must be for the recency of the information contained in the materials.[5]

The second edition of this document describes how collection development should be addressed:

> The school library media program offers a full range of instructional and informational resources that all students need to meet their curriculum goals. Developed in close collaboration with teachers and others, the program's collections reflect the developmental, cultural, and learning needs of all the students. Evaluated and updated regularly, the collections also exhibit accepted and innovative learning theories, effective teaching practices and materials, and current scholarship in the subject areas. Through collaborative collection development and evaluation, the program's collections promote active, authentic learning by providing a variety of formats and activities for linking information literacy with curricular objectives.
>
> With a broad view of the curriculum, extensive knowledge of both traditional and electronic resources, and commitment to serve the full range of students and other members of the learning community, the school library media specialist can direct the design and maintenance of current, comprehensive, high-quality collections.[6]

To follow these suggestions, a good way to begin is with a needs assessment. Start by asking the following questions: What is the *ideal* situation? What are the standards for our type of library? Are they based on traditional or contemporary views? What is *our ideal?* If we could have the library of our dreams, what would it be like? What is *our organization's mission statement and goals?* They should match our personal expectations. Lastly, what are the *expectations and needs* of our outer environment, the community that we serve? Do we understand and appreciate the expectations of our users? Are we responsive to their needs and do we plan accordingly?

After we have asked these questions, the next step is to make an internal analysis of our resources, including all formats. There are several ways to analyze collections, such as focusing on gross numbers, like the overall total, or grouping the collection by classification numbers, or dividing the collection by subject areas, such as those used to support specific areas of a school's curriculum, or even dividing the number of items in the collection by the number of users or potential users to obtain a per capita figure. Collections are often analyzed and quantified by type of material, for example, reference, audiovisual, or special collections. Growth rates can be examined, such as the number of items added or deleted during a year. The expenditures for each type of material during a year may also be considered.

Collections are often compared to published standards for various types of libraries. Often these are only gross numbers, for example, a minimum of ten books per pupil. The problem with these measures is that they are quantitative rather than qualitative evaluations. They tell you how much or how many, but convey little information concerning the quality of the collection.

To get a more qualitative analysis of your collection you could consider comparing your collection to selected lists, such as core collections, or bibliographies for special areas, such as science or college reading lists, or to current adopted textbooks' recommended "further reading" lists, such as those for a new reading series whose purpose is to give students additional practice or reinforcement. Be aware that often these lists are out of date or may not be relevant for your users. You may compare your collection to teacher-generated or other published or recommended bibliographies (such as award lists), analyze by copyright dates (especially useful for topics where the information changes rapidly), analyze by use or lack of use, or have the librarian decide. Use analysis should not rely solely on circulation records because that does not reflect in-house use and is therefore misleading. Analysis by the librarian can be either systematic or impressionistic, for example, judging the physical condition of the material. A combination of these techniques can be helpful, depending upon your objectives. Some suggestions for employing these methods of analysis will be discussed at greater length in later chapters.

The collection is only one aspect of the internal analysis of a library. Other considerations are personnel, facilities, and user perceptions (their levels of satisfaction or frustration either through formal or informal statements). This analysis must also include a community analysis. What kind of community do you serve? What about potential users? What kinds of external resources are there, such as other libraries, museums, agencies, institutions, business, and industry? Consideration of all these elements is useful in preparing an effective collection development policy. Such policies are necessary because they provide guidelines for choosing items for the collection.

One important aspect of analysis that is sometimes overlooked is a personal analysis. You need to put yourself into the picture. What are your career goals? Are you satisfied with the quality of your life? What about your health, both emotional and physical? What about your intellectual and spiritual growth? Are your needs being met? If not, why not? We are well aware of how personal satisfaction affects our job performance. This needs to be taken into consideration.

After you have examined all of these elements, you know where you are and you are ready to develop objectives. By setting and focusing on objectives, you have a plan or a path to follow. You can begin to chart progress. Objectives may fall under daily operations, problem solving, innovation or research, or personal growth and development.

A word of caution is helpful when developing objectives and setting goals. We are often our own worst enemies. We sometimes set goals that take a long time to reach or are impossible to attain or difficult or even impossible to measure. This causes us to become frustrated. We do need to set some long-term goals, but we must also set some objectives that we can attain in a shorter period of time. This allows us to build in our own reward system, to have some positive experiences, to feel good about ourselves, and to continue to strive toward our long-term goals.

After setting our goals and creating objectives, including some that can be measured, we need to develop strategies to meet them. This is a wonderful opportunity to allow the free flow of ideas and to consider alternatives. It is also a wonderful way to collaborate, a primary theme in the new *Information Power.* You might want to try some brainstorming just to bring in some fresh perspectives. The normal constraints of personnel, training, time, hard and soft money, and the effects on users and personnel must be taken into consideration to develop realistic strategies.

The last step is communication and public relations. You need to communicate your goals and objectives to both your inner and outer environment. You need support, encouragement, and involvement from both if reaching your goals is to become a reality.

Why Do a Collection Analysis?

Now that you have an understanding of all the elements that need to be considered in a needs assessment, you may be asking, So what? Why go to all that trouble? What will it accomplish? We have presented the theoretical foundations, but we also know that the approach does work in practice. One of the authors' own experiences as a building level media specialist will be used to illustrate how theory is put into practice.

Several years ago, Pam Barron was the new and the only media specialist at an elementary school in a school district near Columbia, South Carolina. Dan Barron, a professor at the College of Library and Information Science at the University of South Carolina, sent two of his school library administration students out to the elementary school to draw a statistical sampling of the collection.

Based on this sample, the students determined that the average age of the collection was 22.66 years. They also compared this sample to the titles found in Phase 1 of the *Elementary School Library Collection* and discovered that the collection contained only 9.96 percent of the recommended titles.

Until this sample was drawn, the media specialist had sensed that the collection was woefully inadequate, but had no hard data to support this feeling. Building on the students' findings, the media specialist gathered additional statistics. She determined the number of titles needed and the amount of funds required to purchase the remainder of the Phase 1 books. Since a new reading series had just been adopted by the district, she checked to see how many of the supplementary books listed in the series for additional reading practice were in her library's collection. In addition, she isolated one topic, space flight, to examine in greater detail. The results were abysmal.

For example, there were eight titles with the subject heading Space Flight, and their copyright dates were as follows:

1959	1 title
1961	1 title
1963	1 title
1964	1 title
1965	4 titles

This was 1984. Human beings walked on the moon in 1969, but according to the books in this library, they were still trying to get there.

Of the 718 titles listed in the reading series as supplementary books, 56 were in this library's collection. We know that often librarians do not serve on textbook advisory committees, nor are the materials listed always the most recent. Sometimes these lists include only current titles. Still, 56 out of 718 is a poor result.

These data were used to prepare a report for the building level principal. This information was also used by the school's advisory committee to make recommendations to the district administrators. In this school district, each school's budget request was based on recommendations made by its advisory committee. This school's advisory committee recommended that the library's collection be the school's top priority.

After this recommendation was made, Barron compiled a one-page report and made an appointment to talk with the district's assistant superintendent. The actual report that was submitted is presented as figure 1.

The length of the report is important. Administrators are extremely busy and are more willing to give their attention to reports that are concise and that present a clear analysis of the situation. A great deal of information was conveyed to the administrator on this single page. This information also presented facts and clearly documented them rather than just listing impressions. As a result of this report, the administrator decided that additional funding was necessary and assured Barron that steps would be taken before the next school year.

When Barron returned from her summer vacation, she discovered that the administration had given her an additional $1,000. Since she needed almost $8,000, she was, of course,

---

Status of Book Collection at ____________________

The book collection at ______________________________ was analyzed to

1. Determine the age of the collection.
2. Determine the quality of the current collection by making a comparison of titles we have to the titles that should be on the shelves of media centers serving grades K-5. The *Elementary School Library Collection,* a highly regarded selection source, was used to make the comparison.

Results

1. The present collection is 22.66 years old on the average.
2. It contains 9.96 percent of the titles that should be on the shelves of elementary school media centers.

Cost to upgrade the collection to minimum

Nonfiction and Fiction Books	1,746 titles	cost	$12,978.15
Picture Books	687 titles	cost	4,926.76
Total	2,433 titles	cost	$17,904.91

MEMOS

1. The cost of the books listed above reflects the purchase of one copy of a book per title. It does not take into account that multiple copies of some titles would be necessary.

2. These numbers reflect the minimum number of titles that should be included based on recommendations. They do not take into account the supplementary books that are listed for our reading series nor the special collections like the South Carolina books. At present we have 56 of the 718 supplementary books listed for the reading series.

3. Analysis of reference books shows we have 16.67 percent of the minimum number of recommended titles. These books were not included in the costs listed above.

FIGURE 1. Report to a district administrator

badly disappointed. Still she $1,000 more dollars than she would have had if the report had not been written. Rather than give up, she decided to look for additional funding sources.

When school budgets began shrinking, schools started looking elsewhere for funds. One major source of funds for schools has been the business sector. It has become a common practice for schools to form partnerships with local businesses. The businesses adopt the schools and provide them with a variety of resources, ranging from actual products of the company to cash donations. Unfortunately, there were no businesses in this particular school's community that were large enough to lend support. Nor were there any foundations or other philanthropic agencies.

One possible source was the South Carolina State Department of Education. Because of declining test scores, the citizens of South Carolina had agreed to a one-cent sales tax increase to raise funds for education. Also under the terms of the Education Improvement Act (EIA, 1984), grants as large as $5,000 for innovative educational programs, called school improvement grants, were available.

Barron remembered reading an article entitled, "The Effect of Literature on Vocabulary and Reading Achievement," which described a study that had been done to improve the reading skills of children using children's literature.[7] There were many similarities between the student population in the study and Barron's student population; for example, a high percentage of students reading below grade level, low socioeconomic level, and a large minority population. The major difference between these two groups was location. The students in the study were from a large urban area, New York City; the students in Barron's school were in a more rural area. This difference seemed to present a perfect opportunity to replicate the study. Thus, Barron gathered statistics to describe her student population, and she used them in her grant application. She wrote:

> The evidence or need for special emphasis in reading can be found by considering the following background information. Our student body is composed of 402 students in grades K-5.

> Forty-four percent (44%) are reading below grade level. Chapter 1 tutors serve twenty percent (20%). Fifty-five percent (55%) are on free or reduced lunch and thirty-three percent (33%) are from minority groups. While traditional means for teaching reading are good and may meet with some success, many of our students are victims of language impoverishment, due in part to lack of exposure to books. To improve students' reading skills additional strategies for exposing children to books need to be explored.

She submitted a grant proposal, "The Impact of Reading Aloud to 1st, 2nd, 3rd, 4th, and 5th Graders on BSAP and CTBS Scores." These scores are the results of standardized tests used in South Carolina, the Basic Skills Assessment Program (BSAP) and the Comprehensive Test of Basic Skills (CTBS). Figure 2 is a statement of the goals and objectives of the study.

The grant proposal was accepted and the entire grant of $5,000 was used to purchase library books. Ten teachers and 215 students representing two classes for each grade from one to five participated. In each grade level, one class listened to reading aloud for at least twenty minutes per day; the other class did not. At the end of the grant period, an evaluation was made. Test scores had increased. More importantly, this process fostered a greater interest in reading as shown by increased circulation of library books. It also demonstrated to students that they could have pleasurable experiences with books. This observation was based on written responses collected from the participants, both students and teachers. Because of the way grant funds were administered by the South Carolina State Department of Education for that year, the study period was only seven weeks. Barron felt that further study was warranted and the proposal was resubmitted for the following school year. It was funded a second time, and an additional $5,000 was used to purchase library books.

While these grant projects were being conducted, Barron, using the data generated from the collection analysis, was able to get $4,000 for library books from the school's PTA. Thus,

The Impact of Reading Aloud to 1st, 2nd, 3rd, 4th, and 5th Graders on BSAP and CTBS Scores

The purpose of this proposed project is to implement strategies from a successful project conducted in New York City in 1968 which involved elementary school children who had academic retardation, low socioeconomic levels, and a high percentage of racial minorities. The focus of that project was "to find an approach to the problems of poor motivation and inadequate readiness that would stimulate children's desire to achieve competency in reading while strengthening their desire to do so."*

Reading aloud of children's literature was chosen as the appropriate solution to the problem because previous research conducted with children had demonstrated that adults can enhance children's ability to read independently by reading books aloud to them. Results of the project demonstrated that reading aloud to children had a positive effect on word knowledge, quality of vocabulary, and reading comprehension as evidenced by significant improvement on reading achievement test scores. The primary goal of this project is to determine what impact reading aloud to classes of 1st, 2nd, 3rd, 4th, and 5th graders has on their BSAP and CTBS scores.

Measurable outcomes of this project will include:

1. By the end of this project the grantee will develop, use, evaluate, and prepare a list of books that would be appropriate for reading aloud to each of the grades from one to five.
2. By the end of the school year, children in the classes that were read aloud to on a regular basis will show an increase in either their BSAP or CTBS scores over those in the classes that were not read aloud to.

*Dorothy H. Cohen, "The Effect of Literature on Vocabulary and Reading Achievement," in *Jump over the Moon: Selected Professional Readings,* ed. Pamela Petrick Barron and Jennifer O. Burley (New York: Holt, Rinehart, and Winston, 1984), 434-41.

FIGURE 2. Statement of goals and objectives in a grant proposal

one collection analysis was used to generate $15,000 in additional funding, a good payoff for a few hours in work gathering statistics.

South Carolina has had other success stories. Betty Ann Smith, a media specialist in Florence School District 1, effectively used the data gathered from a collection analysis. A news story headlined "School Library Collections Have Outdated Books," in which Mrs. Smith was interviewed, appeared in the *Florence Morning News* on May 3, 1988. It attracted so much publicity that voters passed a bond referendum for library books.

Peggy Hanna, School Library Media Coordinator for the Charleston School District, encouraged all of her media specialists to draw statistical samplings of their collections to calculate the average age. She also told them to select one area of the curriculum for a more thorough analysis. The statistics generated were compiled in a report to the district's administrators. As a result, the libraries obtained additional funding.

We hope these success stories have piqued your interest. The remainder of this book will be devoted to explaining how to draw a sample from your collections and use the data generated to obtain support for your libraries.

For the past twenty years, a great deal of national attention and concern has focused on education and literacy. *A Nation at Risk* helped arouse national concern about American education.[8] Our newly elected president has stated that education is one of his top priorities. As librarians, we are fortunate to be living in a time when the emphasis in education has shifted to collaboration, information literacy, and utilizing the widest array of resources rather than relying solely on textbooks for instruction. Unfortunately, school budgets are being stretched to meet the rising costs of technology. If we are to compete successfully for funding for our library programs, we must use all of the tools available to us. The techniques described in this book have proved to be an effective tool.

NOTES

1. Washington Library Media Association Online at http://www.wlma.org/default.htm. Accessed February 27, 2001.

2. G. Edward Evans, *Developing Library and Information Center Collections,* 2nd ed. (Littleton, Colo.: Libraries Unlimited, 1987), 14.

3. American Association of School Librarians and Association for Educational Communications and Technology, *Information Power: Building Partnerships for Learning* (Chicago: American Library Association, 1998), 113.

4. Phyllis J. Van Orden, *The Collection Program in Schools.* 2nd ed. (Englewood, Colo.: Libraries Unlimited, 1995), 10-12.

5. American Association of School Librarians and Association for Educational Communications and Technology, *Information Power: Guidelines for School Library Media Programs* (Chicago: American Library Association; Washington, D.C.: Association for Educational Communications and Technology, 1988), 72.

6. *Information Power: Building Partnerships for Learning,* 90.

7. Dorothy H. Cohen, "The Effect of Literature on Vocabulary and Reading Achievement," in *Jump over the Moon—Selected Professional Readings,* ed. Pamela Petrick Barron and Jennifer O. Burley (New York: Holt, Rinehart and Winston, 1984), 434-41.

8. National Commission on Excellence in Education, *A Nation at Risk* (Washington, D.C.: Government Printing Office, 1983).

TWO

Gathering and Analyzing Collection Data

It is imperative for school library media specialists to be able to gather and use information about their collections. The purpose of this chapter is to discuss various data that can be readily collected, carefully analyzed, and then used to communicate specific collection strengths to administrators, teachers, students, and other community members.

Automated Systems

Many school libraries today are automated. They have an automated circulation system or an online public access catalog, or both. Sometimes these systems are capable of providing data about the collection. They may generate a report giving the average age of the entire collection or of larger or smaller Dewey classes within the collection. These systems may also generate a report on collection use which details the circulation history of individual titles or groups of titles.

If your library is automated, the first step would be to determine the variety and content of reports generated by that system. It may not be necessary for you to draw a sample and perform data analysis to get the information you need about the collection. Instead, you will need to identify what data your automated system will generate for you. Then determine what those data may mean and evaluate how that information will help you in collection evaluation, collection development, or management of the school library media center.

If your library is not automated or the system will not generate a report containing the information you need, draw a random sample following one of the techniques described below and proceed with the appropriate data analysis.

Sampling the Collection

A library collection consists of books, journals, films, filmstrips, CD-ROMs, pamphlets, and other items. While not actually housed in the library, websites and information available through the Internet are also sources available to users. It is neither necessary nor practical to evaluate every item in the collection. Instead, a small portion of the total collection can and should be used, if that smaller portion is properly selected. This smaller portion, called a sample, can be used to make generalizations about the entire collection.

For the researcher or librarian to make valid inferences about the entire collection, the sample must be representative. That is, the sample must be carefully chosen so it contains all of the characteristics of the library collection and so that those characteristics are present in the same quantity and quality as in the collection itself. For example, if 49 percent of the collection is fiction, then 49 percent of the sample titles should be fiction.

The common method of obtaining a representative sample is to select it randomly. This ensures that every item in the collection has an equal chance of being selected for the sample. Three techniques for obtaining random samples will be discussed later.

Of course, it is impossible for every sample to be a small-scale copy of the collection. Checking a sample of two hundred titles is just not the same as checking every title in the collection. Some differences will occur even when random samples are selected. For example, if a fair coin is tossed ten times, it would be reasonable to predict five heads and five tails. But an actual trial might result in six heads and four tails, or eight heads and two tails. These deviations, called sampling error, that occur when a *random* sample is being selected are due entirely to chance. If the sample is randomly chosen, statistical methods can compensate for sampling error. But they cannot correct for any bias that arises if random sampling is not used. For example, a media specialist may eliminate titles from the sample if she dislikes the author or intends to weed those books shortly. Such bias would adversely affect the final results. Random sampling uses a totally neutral method to identify sample titles. Applied to a random sample, the techniques described in this book can be used with confidence.

Sampling error decreases as sample size increases. One may toss ten heads in a row when using a fair coin. It is much less likely (although not impossible) to toss a fair coin and get one hundred heads in a row. For the techniques described here, a sample size of two hundred titles is recommended. This is large enough to provide useful results (it has been used successfully by this researcher in numerous studies) and it is a manageable size.

When selecting a random sample, the first step is to decide what part of the collection is to be evaluated; for example, circulating items, fiction, nonfiction, nonbook media, periodicals, reference works, vertical file materials, websites, or the entire collection. Before beginning collection evaluation, determine exactly why you want or need to evaluate the collection. This will help identify the area or areas of the collection to examine more closely. For example, in an elementary school which has recently adopted a new reading series for the primary grades, it may be useful to evaluate the picture books. Or, there may be a movement to restrict monies available because the teachers and students now have Internet access. In this case you may wish to both check availability and quality of websites for curricular support *and* evaluate the existing print collection. The answer to the question, "What do I evaluate?" is "It depends."

Once the librarian or media specialist decides what items are to be evaluated, that portion of the collection becomes the population for the study. The next step is to identify a listing of the items where each item is equally represented. For websites, you may use a list of bookmarked sites, sample from a list of recommended sites, or sample from a list of sites generated by a search engine. Some automated circulation systems can generate a list of all titles in their files, and the printout can be used for sampling. It is also possible to sample directly from the monitor screen while scrolling through a listing of all titles and not actually print out a hard copy. (While computers have the capability to generate a set of random titles, at this time automated systems are usually not programmed to do so.) The shelflist (i.e., a listing or set of cards representing every title in the collection and arranged in the same order as titles on the shelves) can be used when one is available. In the shelflist each title is included once, under the main entry, whereas in the card catalog a title may have multiple entries. In a divided card catalog, the title section would be the best alternative if a shelflist is not available. The sample may be taken directly from the shelves if (1) the volumes are counted, not measured (thicker volumes have a greater chance of being selected), and (2) an appropriate proportion of items in circulation is included (see "Stratified Random Sampling," below).

Three methods for selecting a random sample will be discussed here: simple random sampling, stratified random sampling, and systematic random sampling. All three are valid techniques. The most appropriate technique to use depends on the collection and the purpose of the evaluation.

Simple Random Sampling

In this uncomplicated technique, the sample is drawn from the population in such a way that every possible sample of the selected size has the same chance of being chosen. Drawing numbers from a hat and pulling marbles from a jar of equal sized marbles are examples of simple random sampling.

To draw a sample:

1. Identify all items of the library collection from which the sample will be selected. It may be helpful to number the items.
2. *Randomly* select the titles for the sample.

To randomly select the sample, a variety of methods can be used. Tables of random numbers, generated by computer, may be found in math or statistics texts or as separate volumes. These tables can be read in any direction and for as many digits as necessary. Numbers may also be drawn from a hat, or the last digits of phone numbers listed in the white pages can be used. Lists of random numbers can also be generated by computer programs.

In some cases, dice can be helpful, but use them with caution. The familiar pair of six-sided dice does not permit random sampling. The number 1 never occurs, 2 or 12 can only happen in one way, but 1 and 6 or 2 and 5 or 3 and 4 all yield 7. Because each number is not equally likely, a pair of dice cannot be used to select a random sample. But some of the gaming dice for role-playing games have as many as 100 sides, and work well for random sampling.

For an example of simple random sampling, imagine a collection of twelve titles and a sample of 4. Using a random number table, items 11, 2, 9, and 6 were selected for the sample.

x	x
ⓧ	x
x	ⓧ
x	x
x	ⓧ
ⓧ	x

If titles in your identified population have been barcoded, if the barcodes are sequentially numbered, and if you have access to the barcodes and can retrieve items by barcode number, simple random sampling may be the best technique to use to draw your random sample.

Simple random sampling is the least complicated technique. With large collections, it can be unwieldy, and it will not always include members of all subgroups in the collection.

Stratified Random Sampling

If it is important for every subgroup to be proportionally represented in the sample, use the stratified random sampling technique. In this case, a sample is obtained by separating the collection into groups and selecting a proportionate simple random sample from each group.

To obtain a stratified random sample:

1. Identify all items of the library collection to be evaluated.
2. Identify the various groups in the collection to be studied. For example, if all nonreference books in the collection are to be evaluated, and no shelflist or listing of the titles is available, the sample must be taken from books on the shelf and books in circulation.
3. Determine what proportion of the collection is found in each group. For example, you may find 25 percent of the titles are in circulation and 75 percent on the shelf.
4. Decide on the sample size. Two hundred titles are the recommended sample size. For purposes of this discussion, the collection consists of twelve books and the sample size is 4.
5. Calculate how many items of the sample should be allotted to each group. If 25 percent of the collection is in circulation, 25 percent of the sample, or one title, should be drawn from books currently checked out. And 75 percent of the sample, or three titles, should be drawn from books on the shelf.
6. Randomly select the indicated number of titles from each group using simple random sampling. According to a random number table, items 1, 2, and 9 from the first group and item 3 from the second group will be in the sample.

On the Shelf	*In Circulation*
ⓧ	x
ⓧ	x
x	ⓧ
x	
x	
x	
x	
x	
ⓧ	

Stratified random sampling guarantees that all subgroups within the collection, such as the Dewey classes, will be proportionately represented in the sample. But there are times, especially when some subgroups are large, that stratified random sampling also becomes unwieldy. If a list of items in the collection is available, systematic random sampling may be the easiest technique.

Systematic Random Sampling

Using this method, a sample is obtained by selecting items according to a predetermined sequence, such as every tenth book.

To use systematic random sampling:

1. Identify all items in the library collection to be evaluated.
2. Determine the total number of such items in the collection. For purposes of this discussion, the collection size is 12.
3. Decide on the sample size. Again, two hundred is recommended. Four is used in this discussion.
4. Divide the total number of items by the desired sample size to find the interval size. Since 12 divided by 4 equals 3, the interval in this example is 3.
5. Randomly select a starting point less than or equal to the interval. Using the last digits of phone numbers or dollar bill serial numbers can ensure randomness. In this example, the starting point is 2.
6. Starting at the beginning of the list, count to the starting point. That item is the first in the sample.
7. If that item is unacceptable (e.g., it is a reference book and only circulating titles are to be included), continue to the first acceptable item.
8. Add the interval size to the starting place to locate the second title. For example, if item 2 is the first title for the sample and the interval size is 3, then item 5 is the next title in the sample.

9. Continue until the end of the list is reached. Using this technique, items 2, 5, 8, and 11 will be included in the sample.

X X
ⓧ ⓧ
X X
X X
ⓧ ⓧ
X X

This technique can work well if an online circulation system can print a list of all titles in the database. Then systematic sampling can be used to sample from the entire list. This method can also be used to sample directly from a computer monitor if a printout is not desirable or available. Systematic random sampling may also be combined with either of the other two methods. For example, it may be easier to determine the number of pages in the printout than the number of titles listed. In that case, use systematic random sampling to identify pages and use simple random sampling (e.g., throw a role-playing die) to select specific titles.

If the computer printout of holdings is in call-number order, stratified random sampling may determine the proportionate number needed from each of the Dewey or LC classes. Then systematic random sampling may identify specific titles. If the library is not automated, systematic random sampling is an appropriate method for drawing a sample. See appendix A for details on how to sample directly from a shelflist.

The advantage of systematic random sampling is that its orderly approach can be more efficient. If the starting point is selected randomly, the sample is also selected randomly.

Index cards should be used to record the titles in the sample, one title per card. It is much easier to shuffle and rearrange index cards than it is to handle a list of titles on sheets of paper. A format for information on the index card is suggested in figure 3.

As more library collections become automated, fewer shelflists are available. However, each item in the computer

Author ____

Title ____

Call No. ____

Copyright Date ____

Listed in the Standard Source(s):

____

____

____

____

FIGURE 3. Possible format for a sample card

has a unique number or identification code, similar to an acquisition number. Sometimes the computer can print out a list of these numbers or a list of titles held. If the identification numbers were assigned sequentially, and if the beginning and final numbers can be readily identified, then apply the techniques for systematic random sampling.

If neither a computer listing nor a shelflist is available, the sample can be taken directly from the shelves and circulation file. As described before, divide the total collection size by the sample size to find the interval, randomly select a starting point less than or equal to the interval, and, beginning there, select titles separated by the interval, for example, every fourteenth book. Be sure to sample from books in circulation, too. If the circulation file is not accessible, sample from books returned over a period of time.

Data Analysis

The methods of collection evaluation can be either quantitative or qualitative. Quantitative methods attempt to determine collection quality by using numerical data, such as the number of titles in the collection or the average collection age. Qualitative methods attempt to measure the overall quality of the collection.

Comparison to a bibliography of recommended titles or ability to meet user needs can estimate collection quality. Both quantitative and qualitative evaluation can be helpful in analyzing the collection, and both will be discussed here.

Once the random sample has been selected, a number of procedures can be followed to analyze the data. Several of these will be explained and discussed below. Any or all of these procedures may be appropriate in a given situation, and all of them provide additional information about the collection. Use your professional judgment to determine which are appropriate for your situation.

Collection Percentages

It may be useful to know the proportion of titles in various categories or classes of the collection. David V. Loertscher has proposed a method of collection evaluation called mapping (see appendix B).[1] Because this technique relates collection evaluation to the school's curriculum, it is responsive to local needs. Further work by Loertscher and Ho gives data on the percent of titles in different categories for both existing collections and bibliographies of recommended titles.[2] These percentages could be compared with those you obtain to show whether your collection matches the standard data, is below the average in some areas, or is strong in some areas. This information should be used as a guide only. Collections should differ from standard or average data as they respond to local needs. School library media specialists must use professional judgment. Why purchase extensive recommended glacial geology materials if glacial geology is not in your curriculum?

It is possible for some automated circulation systems to list the number of titles in each Dewey class or subclass. It is relatively easy to calculate percentages. See the steps outlined in figure 4. Use the results in a spreadsheet to generate graphs or charts similar to those in figure 5, figure 6, and figure 7. If you sampled from a shelflist to draw your random sample, figure A.2 in appendix A suggests one way to calculate collection percentages.

To calculate the percentage of the collection in each Dewey class:

1. Multiply the number of titles in that category by 100.
2. Divide by the total number of items in the collection. Use the total generated by the circulation system or OPAC.
3. The result is the percentage of the collection in that category. You could enter this into a spreadsheet program to generate a bar graph or pie graph (see figures 6 and 7 for examples).

FIGURE 4. Procedure for calculating collection percentages

Call No.	*No. of Titles*	*Percent*
000s	2	2%
100s	3	3%
200s	3	3%
300s	14	13%
400s	1	1%
500s	21	20%
600s	15	14%
700s	13	12%
800s	4	4%
900s	14	13%
Biog	15	14%
	105	99%

To calculate the percent of titles in each Dewey class in the spreadsheet above:

1. Divide the number of titles in a cell by the total number of nonfiction titles, e.g., 2 divided by 105.
2. Multiply the result by 100.
3. Enter the answer as a percent in the last column.

FIGURE 5. Spreadsheet for percentages of nonfiction titles in Dewey classes

Copyright Dates of the Collection

Once a random sample is available, it can be helpful to use the information to create bar graphs. First, enter the data into a spreadsheet (see figure 8), listing the number of titles per

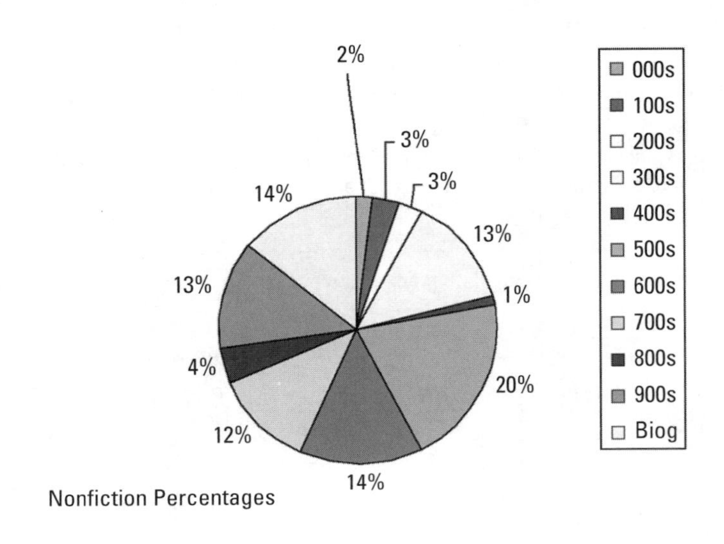

FIGURE 6. Pie graph showing percentages of nonfiction titles in Dewey classes

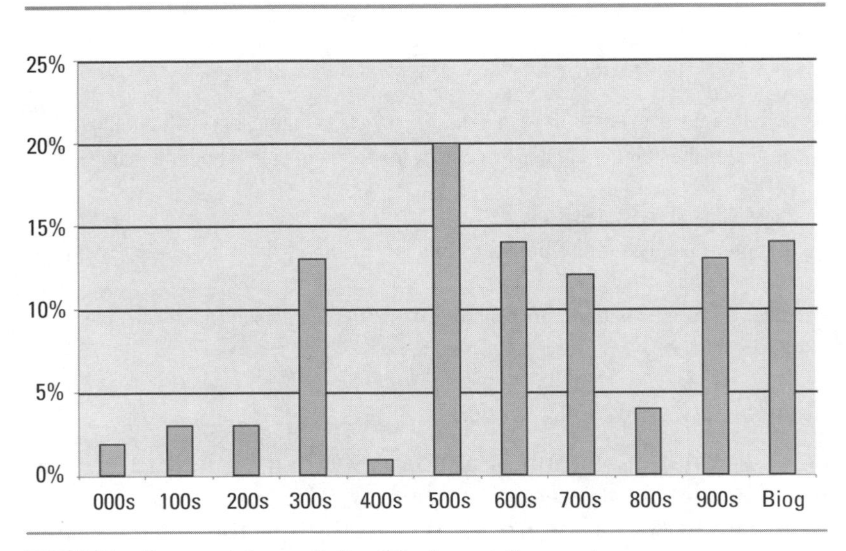

FIGURE 7. Bar graph for nonfiction titles in each Dewey class

Copyright Date	*No. of Titles*	*Fiction*	*Nonfiction*
1955	1	1	
1956			
1957			
1958			
1959			
1960			
1961	1		1
1962	1	1	
1963			
1964			
1965	2	2	
1966			
1967	3	1	2
1968			
1969	1		1
1970	2	1	1
1971	1		1
1972	3	2	1
1973	1	1	
1974	2	1	1
1975	2	2	
1976	2		2
1977	2	1	1
1978	4	1	3
1979	5	4	1
1980	8	4	4
1981	8	3	5
1982	12	6	6
1983	9	5	4
1984	8	2	6
1985	6	3	3
1986	9	3	6
1987	6	3	3
1988	17	10	7
1989	15	5	10
1990	9	4	5
1991	2	1	1
1992	9	5	4
1993	9	3	6
1994	11	6	5
1995	10	5	5
1996	8	3	5
1997	11	6	5
	200	95	105

FIGURE 8. Spreadsheet for sample showing number of titles total, fiction titles, and nonfiction titles by copyright date

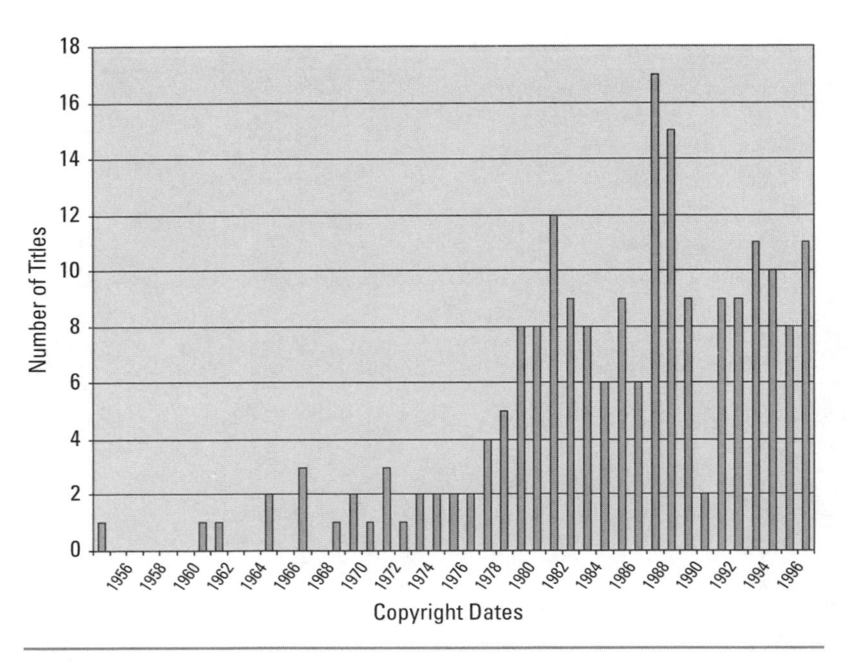

FIGURE 9. Bar graph of copyright dates for sample titles

copyright date. Include all items with copyright dates, such as books, websites, videos, or CD-ROMs. Then the program can create graphs for you (see figure 9). It can also be helpful to separate fiction and nonfiction titles and create a graph that compares the two types of materials (see figure 8 and figure 10).

This graphical representation of the school library media center collection can sometimes help explain the need for new materials better than words alone.

Average Age of the Collection

Another useful number is the average age of the collection. This is also relatively easy to calculate from the sample cards. Using a spreadsheet program, enter the copyright date of each sample title. In this case, you must enter each date rather than

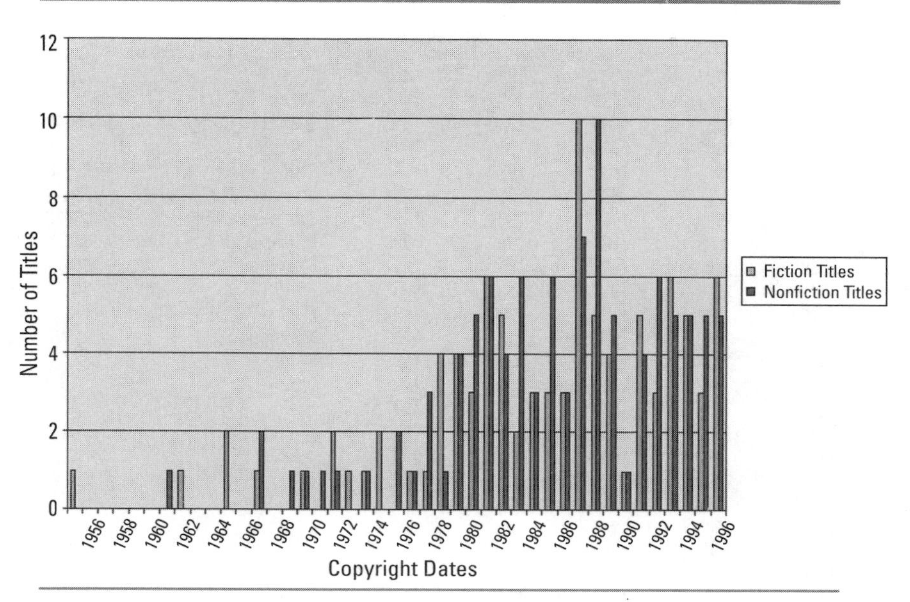

FIGURE 10. Bar graph showing copyright dates of fiction and nonfiction

a total number of titles for each date. For example, 1980 must be entered a total of eight times. Then have the program calculate the average copyright date of the sample (see figure 11). If a random sample was taken, the resulting number identified as the "mean" is the average of the sample, which is also an approximation of the average age of the entire collection or segment of it identified at the beginning of this procedure. You may wish to divide the sample titles into segments and determine the average age of subgroups of the collection, such as fiction or nonfiction (see figures 12 and 13). An alternative technique using a handheld calculator is in appendix A.

There are no definitive data to show how old a school library media collection should or should not be. Some titles written decades ago (classics such as *Wind in the Willows* or *The Tale of Peter Rabbit*) are still valuable in collections; other titles written three or four years ago (such as titles dealing with AIDS) can be outdated. Research shows many school library media collections are twenty to twenty-five years old. Intuitively, this seems

All Titles				
1955	1981	1986	1990	1996
1961	1981	1986	1990	1996
1962	1981	1986	1990	1996
1965	1981	1986	1990	1996
1965	1981	1987	1990	1996
1967	1981	1987	1991	1996
1967	1982	1987	1991	1996
1967	1982	1987	1992	1996
1969	1982	1987	1992	1997
1970	1982	1987	1992	1997
1970	1982	1988	1992	1997
1971	1982	1988	1992	1997
1972	1982	1988	1992	1997
1972	1982	1988	1992	1997
1972	1982	1988	1992	1997
1973	1982	1988	1992	1997
1974	1982	1988	1993	1997
1974	1982	1988	1993	1997
1975	1983	1988	1993	1997
1975	1983	1988	1993	
1976	1983	1988	1993	
1976	1983	1988	1993	
1977	1983	1988	1993	
1977	1983	1988	1993	
1978	1983	1988	1993	
1978	1983	1988	1994	
1978	1983	1988	1994	
1978	1984	1989	1994	
1979	1984	1989	1994	
1979	1984	1989	1994	
1979	1984	1989	1994	
1979	1984	1989	1994	
1979	1984	1989	1994	
1980	1984	1989	1994	
1980	1984	1989	1994	
1980	1985	1989	1994	
1980	1985	1989	1995	
1980	1985	1989	1995	
1980	1985	1989	1995	
1980	1985	1989	1995	
1980	1985	1989	1995	
1981	1986	1989	1995	
1981	1986	1990	1995	
	1986	1990	1995	
	1986	1990	1995	
	1986	1990	1995	

Mean	1985.965
Standard Error	0.569641
Median	1988
Mode	1988
Standard Deviation	8.055946
Sample Variance	64.89826
Kurtosis	1.088894
Skewness	0.961871
Range	42
Minimum	1955
Maximum	1997
Sum	397193
Count	200

FIGURE 11. Spreadsheet showing all sample titles and the average age (mean) of 1985.965. Each year given represents one title.

Fiction				
1955	1987	1997		
1962	1987	1997	Mean	1985.6
1965	1987	1997	Standard Error	0.885291
1965	1988	1997	Median	1988
1967	1988	1997	Mode	1988
1970	1988	1997	Standard Deviation	8.628749
1972	1988		Sample Variance	74.45531
1972	1988		Kurtosis	1.222058
1973	1988		Skewness	1.027433
1974	1988		Range	42
1975	1988		Minimum	1955
1975	1988		Maximum	1997
1977	1988		Sum	188632
1978	1989		Count	95
1979	1989			
1979	1989			
1979	1989			
1979	1989			
1980	1990			
1980	1990			
1980	1990			
1980	1990			
1981	1991			
1981	1992			
1981	1992			
1982	1992			
1982	1992			
1982	1992			
1982	1993			
1982	1993			
1982	1993			
1983	1994			
1983	1994			
1983	1994			
1983	1994			
1983	1994			
1984	1994			
1984	1995			
1985	1995			
1985	1995			
1985	1995			
1986	1995			
1986	1996			
1986	1996			
	1996			

FIGURE 12. Spreadsheet showing fiction titles and the average age (mean) of 1985.6. Each year given represents one title.

Nonfiction

1961	1986	1994		
1967	1986	1994	Mean	1986.295
1967	1986	1995	Standard Error	0.734538
1969	1986	1995	Median	1988
1970	1986	1995	Mode	1989
1971	1987	1995	Standard Deviation	7.526777
1972	1987	1995	Sample Variance	56.65238
1974	1987	1996	Kurtosis	0.721880
1976	1988	1996	Skewness	0.839139
1976	1988	1996	Range	36
1977	1988	1996	Minimum	1961
1978	1988	1996	Maximum	1997
1978	1988	1997	Sum	208561
1978	1988	1997	Count	105
1979	1988	1997		
1980	1989	1997		
1980	1989	1997		
1980	1989			
1980	1989			
1981	1989			
1981	1989			
1981	1989			
1981	1989			
1981	1989			
1982	1989			
1982	1990			
1982	1990			
1982	1990			
1982	1990			
1982	1990			
1983	1991			
1983	1992			
1983	1992			
1983	1992			
1984	1992			
1984	1993			
1984	1993			
1984	1993			
1984	1993			
1984	1993			
1985	1993			
1985	1994			
1985	1994			
1986	1994			

FIGURE 13. Spreadsheet showing nonfiction titles and the average age (mean) of 1986.295. Each year given represents one title.

to be too old, but this is hard to prove. It may be beneficial for you to remind administrators, teachers, and others what was happening in the United States and the world during the year representing the average copyright date of your collection. It may be helpful to determine when curriculum in your school was last revised and use sample data to show the proportion of your collection that supports that update.

For purposes of comparison, a random sample was taken from four retrospective bibliographies listing recommended titles for school and public libraries and the average age for titles listed was calculated. The results are given in figure 14. In writing a report, these average ages could be used as standards and reported with the figure computed for a specific collection. However, these retrospective bibliographies include very few titles that are out of print, and list items that were available

	All Items	*Fiction*	*Nonfiction*	*Computer Science*	*Vocational Guidance*
Children's Catalog (1996)	1984.9	1978.9	1988.1	1994.5	1992.0
Middle and Junior High School Library Catalog (1995)	1986.5	1980.9	1988.36	1993.5	1982.5
Senior High School Library Catalog (1997)	1981.1	1963.9	1989.5	1994.3	1986.8
Elementary School Library Collection (1998)	1989.1 AV 1989.6	1986.7	1990.5	1992.6	1993.0

FIGURE 14. Average copyright date of materials in standard bibliographies

when the bibliography went to press. This policy can result in an average collection age that is younger than necessary, since some useful and formerly recommended titles were out of print when the bibliography was compiled.

Collection Use

Another way of evaluating the collection is by considering its use or potential use. If your media center has an automated circulation system, check sample titles for the circulation records. It may be possible to get the total number of circulations per title or the number of circulations and some idea of when the title circulated. In either of these cases, use a spreadsheet program to generate a bar graph or histogram to show how titles in the collection circulate (see figure 15).

In some cases the automated systems may only list titles that have or have not circulated within a specified time frame (often one year) and perhaps the number of times they circulated. In that case, you have data that reflect use of the entire collection, not just your sample. Use it for a bar graph generated by a spreadsheet program (see figures 16 and 17).

Some automated circulation systems will not give any information about circulation. In that case, use the sample titles, identify the number of those titles currently checked out, and calculate the percentage of titles circulating. The results can be generalized to the entire collection, if the sample was randomly selected.

If circulation is not automated, see appendix A for a suggested procedure to follow using a handheld calculator.

If it is not possible to get circulation information for the sample titles, use the circulation file. The entire set of materials checked out may be used or a sample taken from it. Then, the same types of calculations done for the collection sample, such as average age, should be calculated for the circulating sample. Then the two sets of figures can be compared to identify similarities or major differences. Inferential statistics must be used to identify significant differences.

Copyright	*No. of Titles*	*Titles Circ*	*Not Circ*	*Fiction*	*Fic Circ*	*Fic Not Circ*	*Nonfiction*	*NF Circ*	*NF Not Circ*
1955	1	0	1	1	1				
1956									
1957									
1958									
1959									
1960									
1961	1	1	0				1	1	
1962	1	0	1	1		1			
1963									
1964									
1965	2	1	1	2	1	1			
1966									
1967	3	2	1	1		1	2	2	
1968									
1969	1	0	1				1		1
1970	2	2	0	1	1		1	1	
1971	1	0	1				1	1	
1972	3	1	2	2	1	1	1		1
1973	1	1	0	1	1				
1974	2	2	0	1	1		1	1	
1975	2	1	1	2	1	1			
1976	2	0	2				2		2
1977	2	1	1	1	1		1		1
1978	4	3	1	1		1	3	3	
1979	5	4	1	4	3	1	1	1	
1980	8	6	2	4	3	1	4	3	1
1981	8	7	1	3	3		5	4	1
1982	12	7	5	6	5	1	6	2	4
1983	9	7	2	5	4	1	4	3	1
1984	8	7	1	2	2		6	5	1
1985	6	5	1	3	3		3	2	1
1986	9	8	1	3	3		6	5	1
1987	6	6	0	3	3		3	3	
1988	17	15	2	10	8	2	7	7	
1989	15	15	0	5	5		10	10	
1990	9	8	1	4	3	1	5	5	
1991	2	1	1	1		1	1	1	
1992	9	8	1	5	4	1	4	4	
1993	9	8	1	3	3		6	5	1
1994	11	10	1	6	5	1	5	5	
1995	10	9	1	5	5		5	4	1
1996	8	7	1	3	2	1	5	5	
1997	11	8	3	6	3	3	5	5	
	200	161	39	95	75	20	105	88	17

FIGURE 15. Spreadsheet showing circulation of all titles, fiction titles, and nonfiction titles by copyright date

No. of Circulations	*No. of Titles*	*Percent of Use*
Over 25	29	14.50%
20 to 24	41	20.50%
15 to 19	30	15.00%
10 to 14	17	8.50%
5 to 9	12	6.00%
1 to 4	32	16.00%
None	39	19.50%
	200	100.00%

FIGURE 16. Spreadsheet showing circulation patterns for sample titles

As with collection age, it is possible to divide the sample into fiction and nonfiction titles to compare circulation between these broad categories. It is also possible to follow this procedure for the Dewey subclasses (see figures 18 and 19).

Several of the research articles discussed in chapter 2 presented ways to use circulation data to help in school library media management. Once circulation data are available, the figures can be compared to budgetary spending to check for discrepancies (see figures 20 and 21). For example, if 23 percent of the titles circulated are from the 500s, and only 10 percent of the budget is designated for titles in the 500s, it might be appropriate to readjust that spending. Bertland suggests that circulation figures can be compared to holdings for each Dewey class or subclass to identify areas of high or low usage. Be sure to consider areas emphasized by the curriculum when making these comparisons. It can also be helpful to identify other factors affecting use of certain parts of the collection, such as one teacher inspiring student interest in geology over and above the curriculum.

Comparison to Standard Bibliographies

One method of qualitative collection evaluation is to compare the collection to a standard list of recommended materials. The *Elementary School Library Collection, Children's Catalog,*

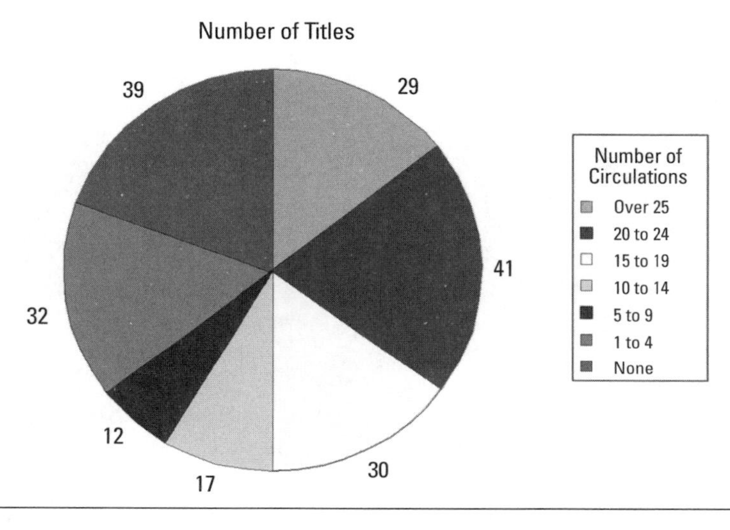

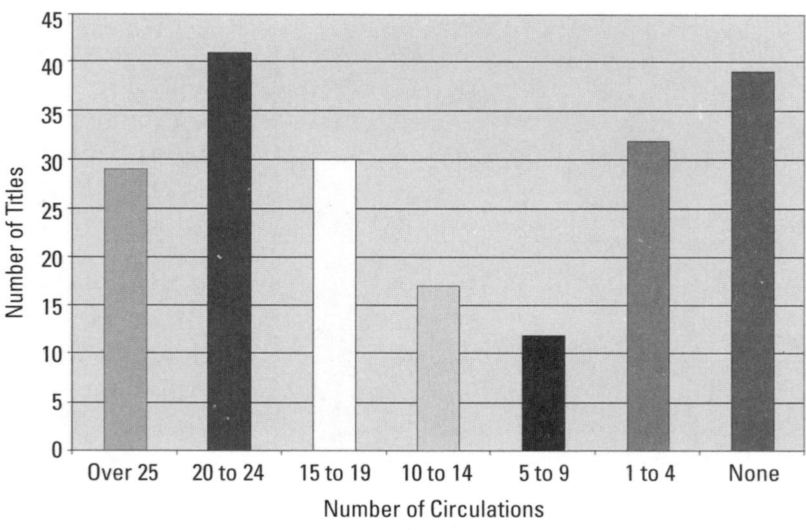

FIGURE 17. Pie graph and bar graph for circulation of sample titles

Middle and Junior High School Library Catalog, and *Senior High School Library Catalog* can be used for this purpose (see "Selected Sources" at the end of this chapter for full information). It is better to use the most recent editions of these titles. Select

Copyright Date	Fiction	Fic Circ	Fic Not Circ	Nonfiction	NF Circ	NF Not Circ
1955	1	1				
1956						
1957						
1958						
1959						
1960						
1961				1	1	
1962	1		1			
1963						
1964						
1965	2	1	1			
1966						
1967	1		1	2	2	
1968						
1969				1		1
1970	1	1		1	1	
1971				1	1	
1972	2	1	1	1		1
1973	1	1				
1974	1	1		1	1	
1975	2	1	1			
1976				2		2
1977	1	1		1		1
1978	1		1	3	3	
1979	4	3	1	1	1	
1980	4	3	1	4	3	1
1981	3	3		5	4	1
1982	6	5	1	6	2	4
1983	5	4	1	4	3	1
1984	2	2		6	5	1
1985	3	3		3	2	1
1986	3	3		6	5	1
1987	3	3		3	3	
1988	10	8	2	7	7	
1989	5	5		10	10	
1990	4	3	1	5	5	
1991	1		1	1	1	
1992	5	4	1	4	4	
1993	3	3		6	5	1
1994	6	5	1	5	5	
1995	5	5		5	4	1
1996	3	2	1	5	5	
1997	6	3	3	5	5	
Total	95	75	20	105	88	17

FIGURE 18. Spreadsheet showing circulation and noncirculation for fiction and nonfiction titles by copyright date

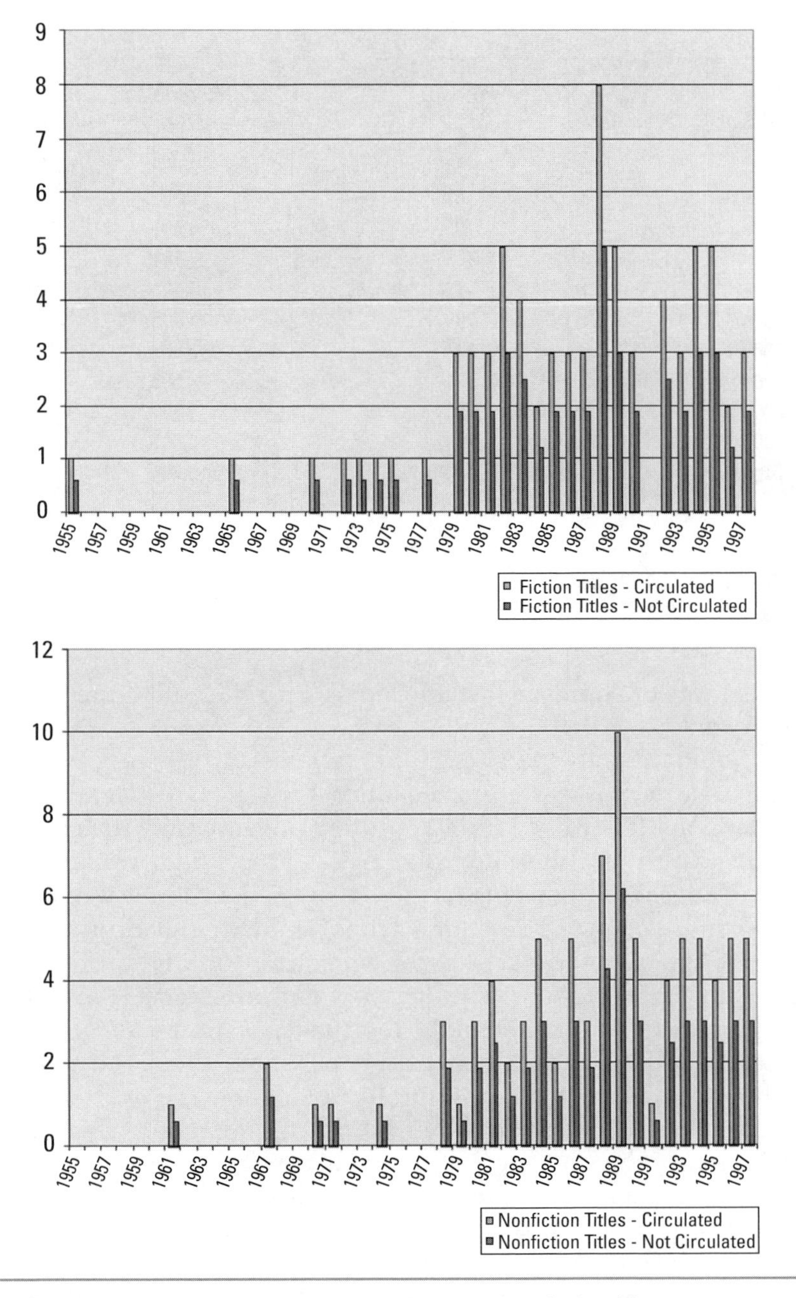

FIGURE 19. Bar graphs for circulation of fiction and nonfiction titles by copyright date

Call No.	*No. of Titles*	*Percent of NF*	*No. of Circ*	*Percent of Circ*	*Percent of Budget*
000s	2	2%	2	2.30%	5%
100s	3	3%	2	2.30%	0%
200s	3	3%	4	4.50%	5%
300s	14	13%	14	16%	15%
400s	1	1%	1	1.10%	0%
500s	21	20%	20	22.70%	10%
600s	15	14%	7	7.90%	10%
700s	13	12%	11	12.50%	10%
800s	4	4%	5	5.70%	5%
900s	14	13%	13	14.80%	20%
Biog	15	14%	9	10.20%	20%
	105	99%	88	100.00%	100%

FIGURE 20. Spreadsheet to compare collection percentages, circulation, and spending for nonfiction titles

the source or sources most appropriate for the collection being analyzed.

Standard retrospective bibliographies can be very useful. They can suggest appropriate titles for school library media collections. They can help in building or evaluating the collection. They represent the collective, professional opinion of knowledgeable librarians or media specialists about which titles could be appropriate for a school library collection.

At the same time, the retrospective bibliographies are generic. That is, the titles suggested are intended for elementary, middle, or high schools any place in the United States. Because of this broad focus, titles pertinent to an individual school, school district, or other local area may be overlooked. Also, these standard lists can be dated, and new titles published after the lists are printed cannot be included. A school library media specialist or librarian must be aware of the specific needs of administrators, teachers, and students in his or her own community or school. Then professional judgment, developed through academic training and personal experience, should be applied to collection development. Each

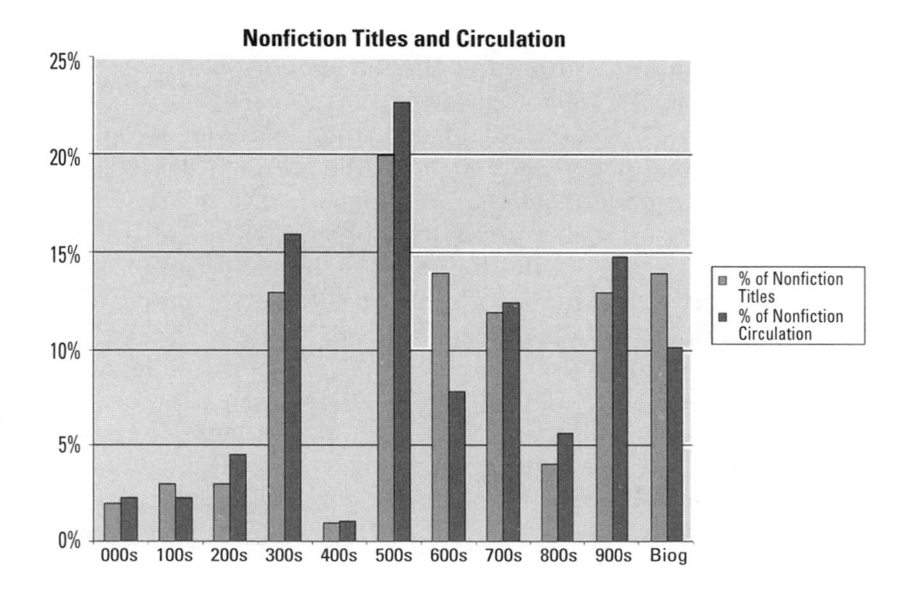

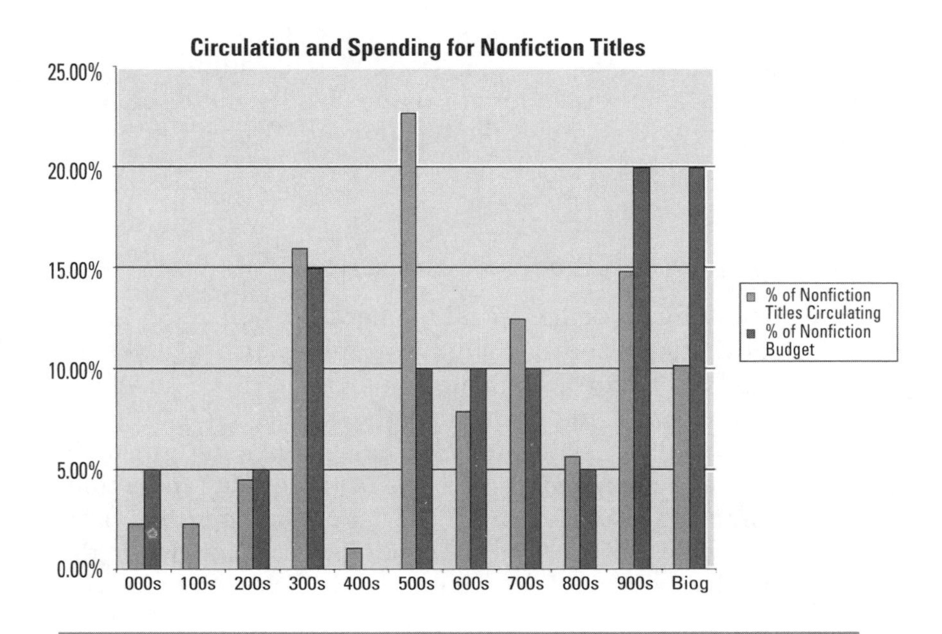

FIGURE 21. Bar graphs showing collection percentages and circulation and circulation and spending for nonfiction titles

media collection or children's collection should be tailored to meet the needs of its school or community.

To estimate the percent of the collection included in the list of recommended materials, first check the sample titles against the list in the standard source. Then separate the sample titles into categories. Using a spreadsheet program, you can determine the percentage of titles found for each segment of the collection or the collection as whole. An alternative procedure, using a handheld calculator, is detailed in appendix A.

This procedure may be used for portions of the collection, such as reference titles, audiovisual materials, or periodicals. If the portion of the collection to be evaluated is large, the sample titles that fall into that category may be used. If the number of titles is more limited, for example, periodicals, all titles in that category may be checked. Figure 22 includes three possible categories and gives directions for calculating the percentage of titles found in the standard source. A selected list of standard sources appears in appendix B.

Other recommended lists of titles can also be used. For example, the Association for Library Service to Children identifies websites appropriate for children. This list could be used to determine how many of the recommended sites can be accessed from your library.

Comparison to Textbooks or Periodical Indexes

In schools it might be beneficial to check the collection to see how many titles listed in the bibliographies of the textbooks being used in the curriculum are available. In this case, check the textbook bibliography against the library collection (as listed in the online catalog or card catalog) and determine how many of the recommended titles are in the library collection. (If the sample is checked against the textbook, the results indicate what percent of the total collection is recommended in the text, not what percent of the recommended titles are in the collection.) Figure 23 suggests a form and a procedure for determining the percentage of titles available.

A. Reference Collection

Source Title ____________________

a. Number of reference books in sample ________

b. Number of titles found in source ________

c. Percent of titles found in source ________

$$\frac{b \times 100}{a}$$

B. Magazine or Periodical Collection

Source Title ____________________

a. Number of magazines in collection ________

b. Number of magazines found in source ________

c. Percent of magazines found in source ________

$$\frac{b \times 100}{a}$$

C. Audiovisual Materials

Source Title ____________________

a. Number of AV items in sample ________

b. Number of AV items found in source ________

c. Percent of AV items found in source ________

$$\frac{b \times 100}{a}$$

FIGURE 22. Comparison to specialized sources

In today's publishing world, titles go out of print very quickly. This means that by the time most textbooks have been adopted by the schools, titles listed in them are often out of print. This shows how important it is for the school library media specialist to be an active member of the school or district curriculum committee.

This same procedure can be used to evaluate how well a periodical collection is supported by the periodical index or electronic database available in the school. Use the list of magazines

Text or index used ______________________

a. Number of titles listed in text or index ________

b. Number of titles found in collection ________

c. Percent of titles found in collection ________

$$\frac{b \times 100}{a}$$

FIGURE 23. Comparison to school textbook/periodicals index

indexed in the reference source as the total number of titles listed; then check the media center's subscription list against the titles indexed. Again, figure 23 can be used to calculate the percentage.

Teacher Requests

In order to document specific areas in the collection that need improvement, it is possible to record teacher requests for curricular materials that the media center is unable to fill. A suggested form is given in figure 24. At the end of a semester these record sheets could be summarized in one report (see figure 31 on p. 52) and included in a report to the principal. This would summarize total numbers only. It may be beneficial to separate the data by Dewey classes or curriculum topics to help identify some specific areas where additional materials are needed. For comparison, or to stress positive aspects of media center service, the same technique could be used to record requests successfully filled.

Evaluation of a Limited Area

Evaluation can have considerable impact sometimes if a limited area of the collection is identified, data are collected, and calculations are done. Care should be taken to select areas which have changed rapidly in recent years or for which having

Teacher's name ____________________

Curricular area ____________________

Material needed ____________________

____

____

Reason unable to supply or slow to obtain material

____

____

____

Will this unit of study be repeated, and the material needed again at a later date?

_________ yes

_________ probably

_________ no

_________ don't know

FIGURE 24. Unmet teacher/curricular need

current information is important. Topics such as computers, geography, health, or careers can quickly become dated. Sometimes larger areas of the general collection are selected for close evaluation, such as materials with Dewey call numbers in the 500s or 600s. The techniques already discussed for the collection in general can also be used with these limited areas. A suggested summary form is given in figure 25.

As with overall collection age, average age of computers and vocational guidance titles have been calculated for several standard tools. These figures can be used for comparison (see figure 14 on p. 33). Be aware of the limitations of these standard sources, as described above.

Figure 26 is a summary sheet. This, or one similar to it, can be used to bring together information in a condensed form. It is often easier for principals, superintendents, and other superiors to digest information presented in this form than it is to study the lengthy calculations performed to arrive at the final figures. Appendix B gives citations to sources for national statistics

Special area of study ____________________

Total number of items included ____________________

Average age of special area ____________________

Amount of use ____________________

Standard source used for comparison

____

Number of items found ____________

Percent of items found ____________

FIGURE 25. Limited areas for evaluation

relevant to school libraries, such as average budgeted materials costs. Such data could be used to support and strengthen conclusions arrived at in analysis of an individual collection.

Estimating Update Costs and Benefits

After a summary sheet like figure 26 has been prepared, it may be necessary to estimate how much it would cost to update the collection. While a precise answer can be difficult to calculate, there are several ways to estimate the cost. Collection age, ability to satisfy teacher requests, or the percent of the collection listed in the standard selection aids or school textbooks could be identified as the areas needing attention. This decision should be based upon the needs of a particular school and the professional judgment of the media specialist or librarian.

Cost of Changing the Average Age of the Collection

If the average age of the collection is the primary concern, the following procedure will give a rough estimate of the amount of money needed to lower the average age of the collection. The procedure should be followed for one type of media at a time. For example, books only could be considered first, and the process could be repeated for CD-ROMs or videos.

1. School name ______
2. Number of students in school ______
3. Annual media center budget ______
   Amount budgeted per student ______
4. Number of titles available in the media center ______
   Number of titles per student ______
5. Growth rate
   - Number of titles added last year ______
   - Number of titles lost/weeded last year ______
   - Number of AV items added last year ______
   - Number of AV items lost/weeded last year ______
   - Number of electronic items added last year ______
   - Number of electronic items lost/weeded last year ______
   - Status of Internet access this year ______
   - Change in status of Internet access since last year ______
6. Average collection age ______
7. Collection circulation figures
   - Percent of collection used this year ______
   - Percent used last year, and not this year ______
   - Percent used before last year and not since ______
   - Percent not used ______
8. Comparison to standard sources
   - Percent found in general source ______
   - Percent found in magazine source ______
   - Percent found in reference source ______
   - Percent found in AV source ______
   - Percent of textbook titles found ______
9. Limited area investigated
   - Total number of items investigated ______
   - Average age ______
   - Amount of use ______
   - Standard source used ______
     - Percent found in standard source ______
10. Number of unmet teacher or curriculum requests ______

School Library Media Specialist ______

FIGURE 26. Summary sheet for collection evaluation

1. Using information from earlier work, fill in the Average Collection Age in the first line of figure 27. This is the current status of the collection and will be used for comparison. Since nothing is being replaced, there is no cost on this line.
2. Decide how many of the older titles you will remove, and then remove a proportionate amount from the sample. If you will replace 5 percent of the collection, remove ten titles from the sample. In that case, the number 10 goes in the first blank on the second line in figure 27.
3. Add items with recent copyright dates into the figures to replace those removed in step 2. For example, if ten older titles were taken out, you may assume that the replacements will have recent dates and, say, add five titles to 1999 and five titles to 2000. This is an attempt to predict the copyright dates of replacement titles. Then calculate the revised average collection age. Enter this number in the blank under Resulting Average Collection Age for the second calculation.
4. To estimate the amount of money needed to raise the average collection age by this amount, use figure 28 and follow the steps given below. You are using the sample data for calculations but need to purchase replacements for the entire collection, not just the sample. So, this procedure is necessary.

	No. of Titles Dropped	*Resulting Average Collection Age (figure 26)*	*Estimated Replacement Cost (figure 28)*
First Calculation	None		None
Second Calculation			
Third Calculation			
Fourth Calculation			
Fifth Calculation			

FIGURE 27. Estimated cost to lower average collection age

	First Calculation	*Second Calculation*	*Third Calculation*	*Fourth Calculation*
a. Number of titles dropped from sample	________	________	________	________
b. Total sample size	________	________	________	________
c. Quotient ($a \div b$)	________	________	________	________
d. Total collection size	________	________	________	________
e. Number of items to be replaced	________	________	________	________
f. Average cost per item	________	________	________	________
g. Estimated replacement cost ($e \times f$)	________	________	________	________

FIGURE 28. Estimated replacement cost

a. Divide the number of titles dropped from the sample (line a) by the sample size (line b). The resulting number (the quotient) should be a decimal (line c).
b. Assuming the same number of titles will be replaced, multiply the entire collection size (line d) by the quotient from line c. The product (line e) is the approximate number of items to be replaced in the entire collection.
c. In line f, enter the average cost for replacing an item. This information is available in the *Library and Book Trade Almanac,* formerly the *Bowker Annual,* and sometimes *School Library Journal.*
d. Multiply the number of items to be replaced (line e) by the average cost per item (line f). The result is the estimated replacement cost (line g).

5. The estimated cost of replacement can now be transferred to the appropriate space in figure 27.

For purposes of comparison, it may be appropriate to repeat this procedure one or more times. It must be stressed that these figures are only rough estimates, and not accurate predictions.

This procedure assumes that if ten items (or fifty items) are removed, ten items (or fifty items) will be purchased to replace them. This may not be true, and could interfere with a media specialist's flexibility. Furthermore, the figure used as the average cost per item is also an estimate. Each replacement item purchased will not cost the same. But the actual average item cost should be fairly close to the estimated average cost. In addition, it is difficult to know exactly the copyright dates of items to be purchased. Recent copyright dates are more probable, but some appropriate older items may be available. Although the estimated cost and revised average collection age are only predictions, sometimes even estimated figures can be appropriate and helpful.

Effect of Expenditures on Average Collection Age

This procedure can be performed in reverse to estimate the impact of a certain amount of funds. For example, a principal may wish to know how much the average collection age would increase if $500 were available for library books.

1. The first step is to use figure 29 to estimate how many sample items would be replaced.
   a. Divide the amount of money available (line a) by the average cost per item (line b). (This information is available in the *Library and Book Trade Almanac,*

a. Amount of money available	________
b. Average cost per item	________
c. Number of items to be purchased ($a \div b$)	________
d. Total collection size	________
e. Quotient ($c \div d$)	________
f. Sample size	________
g. Number of sample titles to be replaced ($e \times f$)	________

FIGURE 29. Estimate of sample items to be replaced

formerly the *Bowker Annual*.) The result is the approximate number of items to be replaced in the entire collection (line c).

b. Divide the number of items to be purchased (line c) by the total collection size (line d). The quotient (line e) should be a decimal.

c. Multiply the quotient (line e) by the sample size (line f) to find the number of sample titles that could be replaced with the money available (line g). In cases where a decimal results, round to the nearest whole number. For example, 5.1 becomes 5 titles and 6.7 would be interpreted as 7 titles. Record the results in figure 30.

2. Returning to the spreadsheet program used to calculate average collection age, subtract the estimated number of items to be replaced from items belonging to the earlier years on the chart. Then add that number of titles to the items belonging to the more recent years. For example, if 10 items may be replaced, remove 10 of the older items. Then add five titles in each of two recent years, e.g., 1999 and 2000.
3. Following the procedure given for calculating average collection age, recalculate the average collection age using these new figures. Enter the results in figure 30.

This procedure gives only an estimated or predicted change in average collection age. It does not guarantee accurate figures and is subject to the same constraints and concerns discussed for the cost of changing the average age of the collection. However, there are times when this procedure can be

Amount of money available	__________
Number of sample titles dropped (figure 29)	__________
Resulting average collection age	__________

FIGURE 30. Estimated effect of money on average collection age

helpful. It may be useful to repeat the procedure for various amounts of money.

Satisfying Teacher Requests

The media specialist, principal, or school district may be concerned about the ability of the library collection to meet the curricular needs of teachers. Figure 31 is proposed as one way to keep track of teacher requests that the collection cannot supply at the present time. (Figure 31 can be used to summarize data recorded using figure 24.) It may be beneficial to separate the data by Dewey classes or subject areas to help identify some specific areas where additional materials are needed or to separate by type of material, for example, reference, periodicals, or electronic. For comparison, or to stress positive aspects of media center service, the same report could be used to record requests successfully filled.

To estimate the cost of improving the collection's resources to satisfy teacher's needs, use figure 32 and the following procedure.

1. Decide which items will be purchased. This could be determined according to subject (e.g., science), type of material (e.g., books), or a combination of both (e.g., science books). It may be appropriate to consider whether or not the material will be needed next semester or next year

	Will it be needed again?			
Material	*Yes*	*Probably*	*No*	*Don't Know*
Books	______	______	______	______
Audiovisual materials	______	______	______	______
Electronic materials	______	______	______	______
Periodicals	______	______	______	______
Reference materials	______	______	______	______

FIGURE 31. Number of unmet teacher/curricular needs

and count only items that probably will be used again. The media specialist must use her knowledge of the curriculum and personal experience to determine which items to include. Once the decision has been made, the type of title, such as science books, is to be written in the first column of figure 32. The number of items proposed for purchase belongs in the second column.

2. Using the *Library and Book Trade Almanac,* formerly the *Bowker Annual,* or some other source, enter the average cost per item in the third column.
3. Multiply the number of items to purchase by the average cost per item to estimate the cost of purchasing these items.

The number calculated estimates the cost of purchasing all of the identified items. Because there is no sampling involved in this procedure, the number of items and the resulting estimated cost are directly related. For example, if only half of the identified items are purchased, the corresponding estimated cost will be half as large. If 10 items would cost $90, then 5 items would cost $45. That is, if one is changed by multiplication or division, the effect on the other figure can be determined by multiplying or dividing it in the same way.

It must be remembered that the cost calculated is an estimate. The items purchased will not all cost the same, but the actual average should approximate the average from the *Library*

Type/category of item to be purchased	______	______	______
Number of items to be purchased	______	______	______
Average cost per item*	______	______	______
Estimated cost	______	______	______

*This information can be obtained from the *Library and Book Trade Almanac.*

FIGURE 32. Estimated cost of meeting teacher needs

and Book Trade Almanac. Probably not all the items requested by the teachers will be available for purchase, and the teachers will have new requests next year. But this procedure should estimate some of the costs to improve the capability of the collection to meet teacher's curricular needs. Of course, it is possible to use *Books in Print* or publishers or jobbers catalogs or websites to identify specific prices.

Comparison of Information in Various Formats

Today, information is available in a wide variety of formats. Each format has specific strengths and weaknesses. School library media specialists have training in looking at and evaluating many of these formats. Which format or formats are suitable for a particular topic depends on the topic and on the formats. In schools, our students are usually best served by exposure to as many formats as possible.

Sometimes it may be difficult to convince ourselves, teachers, principals, and students that more than one type of information format is necessary. For example, some people are saying that with information available on the Internet we don't need books anymore. One way to counter that argument is to select a topic, locate information in a variety of formats for that topic, and then compare the information found. Use (or adapt to your local situation) the chart in figure 33 and the procedure outlined below.

1. Identify a topic to investigate. This topic may be curricular or deliberately selected to showcase poor or strong sources. Possible topics might be zoo animals, sources of alternative energy, or African-American history. Write the topic in figure 33.
2. Locate information available on the topic in as many formats as possible. It may be appropriate to limit the search to resources available in the school library media center or in the community, or to search as widely as possible to find an exhaustive set of information. The decision of how extensively to search depends on the

Topic ______		
Item	______	______
Format	______	______
Currency	______	______
Depth of coverage	______	______
Authority	______	______
Ease of use	______	______
Locatability	______	______
Permanence	______	______
Ownership/Access	______	______
Unique characteristics	______	______

FIGURE 33. Comparison of information in various formats

reason for doing this exercise and what will be done with the final information. Possible formats include (but are not limited to) books; journals and journal articles; videos; audiotapes; pictures, maps, charts or other graphics; CD-ROMs; realia; and websites. Write the items and the types of formats located in the spaces in figure 33. Add more spaces if necessary.

3. Now look at and evaluate the information in the items you have located. Some areas for evaluation are discussed here. Add more if appropriate to your situation.

Currency. How recent is the information available in this item? The importance of currency varies with the topic selection. For example, information on AIDS needs to be current; information on American history is less time-sensitive.

Depth of coverage. How much information is available in this source? Some sources, like almanacs, give a lot of quite shallow information. Other sources, such as books or videos, may choose to explore one topic in great depth. At times too much information can be just as bad or worse than too little information. So, evaluate each item in terms of appropriate coverage of the topic for the students and the curricular need identified.

Authority. How trustworthy is the information? For example, a website on cancer mounted and maintained by the American Cancer Society has more authority than one which is anonymous.

Ease of use. How much effort will it take for students or teachers to find the information they need? Some of the ease of use is a function of the format (e.g., it can be difficult to locate a specific incident in a video); some is a function of the item itself (e.g., a book index may be well done or poorly done); some is a function of the user (e.g., students who cannot read will have more difficulty with some formats than with others).

Locatability. How much effort would it take students or teachers to locate the information found? For example, searching for information on the Web can be a convoluted, frustrating, and time-consuming process. Some students use OPACs easily; other students have difficulty using them. Items in the school media center would presumably be easier to find than items in a local university collection.

Permanence. How durable is this information? Once the school library media center owns a book, it will be in the collection until lost or weeded. A website can disappear overnight, however. Items physically located in the school library media center can be located even if access to the Web is temporarily interrupted. Information from a district center or public library could probably be faxed to the school.

Ownership/Access. Does the school library media center own this item? Or is it leased or available through another library in the community or through the Web. Ownership may be the most "durable" form of access, but items can be lost, stolen, or weeded. Items available through other agencies may continue to be available long term, depending on the agency and any agreements that may or may not be in effect with the school library media center. Items that are licensed or leased, such as databases, may no longer be available if the lease is not renewed. And, as we all know, websites can change addresses, move, or disappear overnight.

Unique characteristics for this format. What are the unique characteristics or special features of this item particular to this format? And is that characteristic important for the topic chosen? For example, videos can show motion. CD-ROMs can provide random access and sound, so can be ideal to help students identify songs of specific birds.

4. Fill in figure 33, creating as many blanks as necessary. It may be possible to quickly evaluate all of the items located, or it may be appropriate to examine only a few of the items located. If only some of the items located are evaluated, be sure to take a random sample if you wish to generalize back to the entire population of items available.

The information gathered can be shared with teachers, administrators, students, and parents to help explain the role and function of having a wide variety of formats available for curricular support. It can help to clarify some of the issues around quantity and quality of materials available through the school library media center.

Conclusion

In this chapter you have been given a variety of techniques for analyzing the data collected in your sample. Once you have clarified your objectives, it is simply a matter of utilizing the data to your advantage.

NOTES

1. David V. Loertscher, "Collection Mapping: An Evaluation Strategy for Collection Development," in *Measures of Excellence for School Library Media Centers,* ed. David V. Loertscher (Englewood, Colo.: Libraries Unlimited, 1988).

2. May Lein Ho and David V. Loertscher, "Collection Mapping: The Research," in *Measures of Excellence for School Library Media Centers,* ed. David V. Loertscher (Englewood, Colo.: Libraries Unlimited, 1988).

SELECTED SOURCES

Bowker Annual: Library and Book Trade Almanac. 46th ed. (New Providence, N.J.: 2001).

Homa, L. L., ed. *The Elementary School Library Collection: A Guide to Books and Other Media, Phases 1-2-3.* 21st ed. Williamsport, Pa.: Brodart, 1998.

Price A., and J. Yaakov, eds. *Children's Catalog.* 17th ed. New York: H. W. Wilson, 1996.

———. *Middle and Junior High School Library Catalog.* 7th ed. New York: H. W. Wilson, 1995.

Yaakov, J. *Senior High School Library Catalog.* 15th ed. New York: H. W. Wilson, 1997.

THREE

Weeding

What Is Weeding?

Many people have difficulty throwing anything away. Librarians are no exception. Most librarians will agree that it is sometimes necessary to remove items from a collection, but that does not make the task any easier. Weeding is an essential but often overlooked aspect of collection development. It is essential because it helps to improve access to a library's resources. Every library has a finite amount of space that can be used to house its resources. Library collections should always be evolving to reflect changes in the information needs of its users and changes in the information itself. Weeding affords librarians the opportunity to reevaluate their collections

Weeding is sometimes thought of as selection in reverse because it removes resources from the collection when they are no longer useful. It involves evaluation of the collection in order to determine which resources need to be removed from the collection. This process has been described as retirement, pruning, reverse selection, deselection, relegation, and discarding. Since all of these terms have negative connotations, it is sometimes difficult to convince administrators and users that this is an important function, especially since some collection evaluation standards are based on the total number of items in the library rather than quality or relevancy. We need a more positive term to describe this process because it is an essential aspect of collection management. One suggestion is to try the term used by the Washington Library Media Association. They call it *collection renewal.* Another suggestion is the term *collection reevaluation.* Both of these are more proactive and positive concepts. They imply management, professionalism, and decision making.

No matter what we choose to call it, a good working definition is important. One definition is the process of removing materials from a collection to another location. That location does not necessarily mean a trash can, but it could be a secondary storage site, another library or institution, or a book sale. No matter what kind of secondary site is chosen for the disposal of the material, that material is no longer immediately accessible to users.

Stueart makes the point that weeding and discarding are sometimes used interchangeably, but in fact are not synonymous.[1] According to the definition given, storage is an optional aspect of weeding. Storing enables the library to retain the material but at a second level of access usually not open to the public. It serves as an interim solution because libraries have a finite amount of storage space.

Now that we have a working definition, it is time to take the next step. The professional literature about weeding stresses the importance of planning so that decisions are based on facts, not whims or hunches. Before any program is implemented, the library's goals need to be reevaluated to ensure that the materials being weeded will be those that are no longer relevant to the library's collection.

Evaluation of Policy and Goals

Collection reevaluation (weeding), though essential, can be one of the most controversial aspects of collection development. Formulation and adoption of policy are a necessity. The new standards for school library media centers as set forth in *Information Power* address the importance of policy formulation in collection development. "All schools must have a collection development plan that addresses their collection needs and includes such specific steps as school and community analysis, policy development, selection, acquisition, weeding, and evaluation."[2] Note that weeding is seen here as an important aspect of collection development. Unfortunately, this statement does not appear in the revised version published in 1998. The new version simply reads "The collections of the library media program are developed and evaluated collaboratively to support the school's curriculum and to meet the diverse learning needs of students."[3] There is no mention of policy with regard to collection development anywhere in this new document. This is a serious oversight. Selection of materials and weeding are similar activities; they require the same kinds of decision making. The key concepts in collection development, just as in collection analysis, are management and planning.

In establishing a weeding program, Stueart cautions, "to reduce the hazards implicit in weeding, three essential steps should be included in the initial planning process: (1) analysis of needs, (2) analysis of options, and (3) determination of what is feasible."[4] His article, despite its date of publication, presents a comprehensive overview of the topic and addresses many of the most common concerns about the process, such as reasons for weeding, for example, redundancy in the collection; shifts in goals and emphases of the library; physical deterioration or obsolescence of materials; and, the need for space. He also discusses several points that need to be considered in developing a weeding strategy, such as cost, politics, the availability of storage, and cooperative agreements. To this list we now need to add electronic access. With the emergence of the Internet, many resources are available to us beyond the physical confines of our libraries. We also have a wide array of electronic formats. Access now has a much broader scope than ever before. To avoid problems, there is much to consider, such as checking to see if there are any local constraints, regulations, or statutes that might affect your weeding program or laws that might prohibit the sale of books.

Phyllis Van Orden raises some interesting points for consideration in developing a policy for reevaluating items in your collections to determine which items should be repaired, replaced, or removed.[5]

1. What will happen if someone needs the materials that have been removed?
2. How can we provide a replacement policy to assure that a decrease in numbers of items held will not lead to a budget cut?
3. What will the source of funding be for the cost of the reevaluation if additional personnel are needed?
4. How will the transfer or disposal of materials and equipment be handled?

By considering these and other factors, you can form or review your collection development policies and goals. After a policy is in place, you must translate it into action. Most of us are not able to go through our collections from one end to the other, so it is useful to consider other strategies. Oftentimes we have space problems in a specific area of our collection or subjects have been added to or deleted from the curriculum. Then it is useful to identify priorities or areas of immediate need to establish a schedule for weeding. It is important to consider what is feasible with the staff available, the structure of the weeding program, and the establishment of a timetable. We need to decide whether or not we will opt for continuous weeding as materials are returned, or intermittent weeding throughout the year, or occasional weeding as part of a day or for a whole day. Unless we make time for it, it will not get done.

In Defense of Weeding

Weeding is one aspect of collection development, and a natural follow-up to collection evaluation. Weeding occurs when materials no longer appropriate for a collection are removed from it. While many librarians and media specialists acknowledge the need for and value of weeding, parents, teachers, and administrators and other users do not always understand. The following reasons for weeding can both stimulate the professional's own thinking and can explain weeding to others.

There are a number of reasons why librarians should remove materials from the shelves of their collection. They include rapidly growing collections combined with a shortage of space, the high costs of maintaining and adding shelving space, the need to maintain both accuracy and currency in information, the need to improve access to information for users, and the problems created by physical damage to the materials.

An incredible amount of resources are available in print and electronic formats. Even with the self-imposed limitations on the numbers and types of items obtained because of budget constraints, most libraries are still accumulating materials at a rapid rate. This means that more and more items are being added to library collections. Each item needs to be cataloged and shelved, and each takes up space.

Space can soon become a severely limiting factor. Every inch of shelving and storage space costs money, not only to build and put into place, but also to maintain. Buildings are not easily expanded, and there are only so many clever compact-shelving ideas available. All options generally cost money.

We have a professional responsibility to provide our users with the best resources possible. Any resource that does not include the most recent information is not likely to be of value to our users. At best, it is simply not useful; at worst it is dangerously false.

Further, as collections grow and new resources become interspersed with older ones, the ability of the users to locate the best source possible becomes increasingly limited. Many users do not have the patience to wade through too many inaccurate or outdated materials to locate the one valuable resource. Removal of the obsolete material makes it easier and quicker for the user to locate what he or she needs. Most people take the path of least resistance and do not expend a lot of energy looking.

Information in some materials may be inaccurate or dangerous, perpetuate stereotypes, or somehow contain misinformation. Too frequently, biographies for children have errors, as Moore shows clearly in her article.[6] Some science-fair books instruct children to build a volcano using matches instead of baking soda and vinegar. Chemistry books may advocate dangerous experiments. Some books do stereotype minorities, women, the aged, or other groups in ways that are clearly inappropriate. The media specialist or librarian can justify removing these materials.

Some of the materials in a library collection, either through normal usage or borrower carelessness, become damaged. They may be dropped in a mud puddle, chewed by the dog, or colored by helpful hands. Pages may be torn or missing; the binding may no longer hold the book together; the cover may fall off. The VCR (videocassette recorder) may mangle a videotape; a CD-ROM may become badly scratched, etc. The types and causes of damage are many and varied. Some items can be repaired. Others may need to be weeded.

Library users and their needs change. Changes in technology have rendered some formats, such as filmstrips, obsolete. Therefore, a library collection must also change if it is to continue to meet the needs of its users. Some of this can be accomplished by purchasing new items. But it is also helpful to remove items that are no longer pertinent.

As materials are removed from the collection, there can be a number of positive outcomes. For example, weeding can relieve overcrowding and make space available for new acquisitions. Access to the remaining materials can be greatly improved because it is easier to find an item if there are fewer materials to search. Often, the weeded collection will become more physically attractive. As its appearance improves, users may begin to have more respect for items in the collection and therefore treat them more carefully.

The number of items in a collection by itself is not a good indicator of its quality. Other factors, such as age, currency, and accuracy of the content of items in the collection must be considered. At the same time, standards and regulations may rely on collection size as an indication of quality. Weeding the collection helps decrease reliance on numbers alone, and can improve the overall collection by removing substandard items.

Weeding can be cost-effective. There are continuing costs associated with maintaining a library collection. Besides the ordinary costs of heating, cooling, and so forth, there are specific activities associated with the collection. Shelves must be read to keep materials in the proper order. Items must be dusted and kept clean. All materials should be inventoried regularly. The public access catalog and an inventory must be maintained. It is a drain on library resources to perform these activities for items that no longer belong in the collection.

As technology improves and becomes more affordable, most libraries have converted to online catalogs and circulation systems. It is not efficient to spend time and money entering materials into the new system when those items no longer belong in the collection. Therefore, weeding should be done before automating the library or media center.

Barriers to Weeding

In weeding, the same steps that placed materials on the shelves are performed in reverse. It is a time-consuming effort. Our professional literature is filled with reasons, rationalizations, and excuses for why we do not weed our collections. The following are the reasons most frequently cited.

1. *I am too busy. I have no time to weed.*

   We would find the time if we knew how much it costs us to house an obsolete item.

2. *Books are sacred.*

   We have emotional and intellectual blocks against removing books from a collection. Many of us consider books to be valuable records of our human heritage. Removing them becomes painful.

3. *A book might be needed by someone at some time in the future.*

   This is rare. It is much more likely that you will be asked for a book that you never acquired. Few libraries, even the large research libraries, can afford to house a book until sometime in the future when someone shows up to use it. A more realistic approach is to consider cooperation and networking with other libraries. Make agreements about what will be collected and kept by whom.

4. *Numbers are considered a criterion of the quality of a library.*

   We are forced to play a numbers game and include obsolete items in the official count. Unfortunately, quantity is no indication of quality. A good library is not necessarily a big library.

5. *I hate to admit that I made a mistake in selecting this item.*

   So what? Because selection is not based on scientific formulas or objective measurements, but rather on the librarian's judgment of resources and people, every librarian has probably made some mistakes. There were all sorts of variables at work when that item was selected, i.e., how much money you had, interest in the subject at that time, availability of other titles on the same subject, etc. You can sharpen your judgment by experience and training, but you can never make it infallible.

6. *Weeding is just willful destruction of public property.*

   No, it is a very constructive process, as outlined in the next section.

General Guidelines for Weeding

Given that weeding is an integral part of collection development, decisions on whether to retain or remove an item must be made on an individual basis. There is no easy-to-follow rule or set of rules to use in making each decision. Instead, each librarian or media specialist must apply professional judgment and a thorough knowledge of the user community when weeding the collection. However, there are some general guidelines that may be helpful.

The physical condition of an item may be reason for removal. It may be so battered, torn, dirty, or damaged that it is not worth the time and effort needed to recondition it. Small print, missing pages, or any damage to or obsolescence of electronic formats are indicators for removal.

Duplicate copies can be justified for items that are in great demand. As use declines, the extra copies can become candidates for weeding. Other changes in user needs, such as curriculum revisions and changes in the demographics of the user population, can result in decreased use of some items in the collection. If Latin has not been taught in a school for the last twenty years, does its media center still need thirty titles in Latin?

With time, the utility of some items decreases, and it may be appropriate to remove them from the collection. It is reasonable to question the value of a set of encyclopedias published in 1953. Published guidelines, such as those in Van Orden's book, are available, which suggest appropriate ages or circulation data for weeding different subject areas and various types of materials.[7] For other items, the content may be superseded by newer editions or recent developments, in addition to the general age guidelines. If a new edition is published, does the collection really need two earlier editions? There are some fields, such as space flight, which change very rapidly. Older titles in these areas should be checked for obsolescence and removed when they become dated.

There are materials in any library collection that do not belong there. Some items are not being used, either in or out of the library. The library users may have changed. If the media center originally served kindergarten through sixth grade, but now the users are primary-grade children, then many books on the fifth- and sixth-grade reading levels may no longer be needed. The demographics of the community might have changed and the collection does not reflect this new cultural diversity. There may be unsolicited gifts in the collection that do not meet the criteria in the selection policy. Some items may have been acquired through mistakes in selection. Any materials that are inappropriate for a particular collection are candidates for removal.

For some items, initial purchase is justified. These include the local newspapers and magazines of special interest to users. But if these are not indexed, there is little need to keep many back issues. Without access, information in these items is almost impossible to locate. So it is better to use available storage for magazines, newspapers, and other items where it is possible to find specific articles or other content easily.

General Guidelines for Retention

The comments given above are intended as general guidelines only. The professional judgment of the librarian or media specialist must be used throughout the entire procedure. When a decision is made about removing an item, that decision may be guided by the rules of thumb given here. But the librarian's personal experience, knowledge of availability of resources in a wide variety of formats, access to information resources, and familiarity with the users are also vitally important.

Just as there are some materials that should be weeded, there are some items that should be retained in a collection, such as items that are still being used by a particular user or user group. One book, for instance, may be especially adept at introducing children to an idea or stimulating discussion. That title is important to the adults who continue to use it with children. When useful items are identified, and if they are out of print or otherwise unavailable, they probably should not be discarded. In this case, even older or worn titles may need to be retained.

It is important to be aware of the overall balance of the collection. If removing materials would impair collection coverage in a particular subject area, it may be better to retain the items. Sometimes it is possible to have certain titles rebound. Other repairs may help extend the life of certain materials.

In general, the classics have a place in children's collections. Unless a newer, more attractive edition is available, those titles should be kept. Also, within the bounds of professional judgment, it may be valuable to retain items listed in a current edition of a standard bibliography for a particular library.

Some materials are of special interest to an individual library. These may include titles about local or state history or peripheral items pertinent to individuals or groups in the community. Local publications, such as school yearbooks, can be of interest. These items can be difficult or impossible to replace, and are often of continuing interest or importance. They should be retained in the collection, unless they are available elsewhere in the community. (For example, newspapers often keep their own back files of publications.)

Some items may be of interest to a particular library. For instance, a prominent local author may present autographed copies of his books to the library. Titles purchased with memorial funds may fall into this category. There may be an occasional rare book. These items may need to be retained. If such an item is identified it may be helpful to prominently stamp it, "Do not discard."

There are no ironclad rules for weeding. There are only general guidelines to help the librarian or media specialist apply professional judgment. A very helpful resource called *Sunlink: Weed of the Month Club* has been developed by the Florida Department of Education School Library Media Services Office. *SUNLINK Weed of the Month Club* maintains a website to help media specialists and librarians weed their collections.[8] Monthly topics are identified for consideration, and specific criteria and considerations for each topic are listed, along with titles recommended for weeding and titles recommended for use. The current topic (September 2001) is conflict management. These topics are still available through their website: immigration, civil rights, poetry, nutrition, science experiments, curiosities and wonders, tobacco education, Cuba, drug and alcohol education, transportation, black history, music, hobbies and crafts, weather, professional collections, vocational trades, personal finance, maps and atlases, sports, holidays, geography, fiction, computer science, folktales, biography, cookery, dinosaurs, diseases, careers, Europe, Africa, Native Americans, and space and astronomy. It is an invaluable resource.

How to Discard Library Materials

Once you have actually removed items from your collection, you are faced with having to get rid of them. This can sometimes be a ticklish situation, and horror stories abound concerning discarded items that return to flaunt their original owners. You need to develop a plan based on your own situation. The following list of methods that have been tried comes from Iowa's Department of Public Instruction:[9]

1. Bag and tag for destruction.
2. Put a few in each waste basket every day.
3. Take them to the dump.
4. Take them to another community's dump.
5. Tear or break them up and put them in a waste basket.
6. Offer them to a charity book sale—many such groups now sell magazines, records, etc., as well as books.
7. Have a white elephant sale.
8. Offer other libraries or other agencies in the community an opportunity to select anything they can use.
9. Box and send them to the superintendent.
10. Store them until they are forgotten.

Another recent suggestion is to sell them on the Internet on Ebay. Before doing so, check out the legal implications. You also need to make sure that you are not selling something that has become highly collectible. If you still want to sell it, make sure you get fair market value for it.

The same publication offers some important points to consider when selecting a method.[10] (Note: These points are applicable to most libraries.)

1. The method(s) selected should be in harmony with school policy.
2. The school district selection policy should specifically assign responsibility for discarding library materials and equipment to the library media specialists, including responsibility to determine intrinsic worth.
3. The school district should use established depreciation tables for library materials and equipment. Such tables

also help justify discarding materials and equipment purchased with general funds.

4. All items not destroyed should have all identifying marks removed or be clearly marked as discarded.
5. Library materials in classrooms need to be weeded too. The classroom should not become a dump. If older items such as sets of encyclopedias are placed in the classrooms they should be discarded after a specified time, such as ten years.
6. If major weeding is to be done, the school and community should be prepared and advised that regular weeding in the future will be at a more sedate pace.

The comments made about classrooms in point 5 are especially relevant to school media specialists. If teachers have large personal collections of resources in their classrooms, they may be hesitant to allow students to visit the media center.

This final point is an important one. It is imperative to win weeding supporters in order to avoid a public relations nightmare such as the one that happened at the San Francisco Public Library, when more than 100,000 volumes were discarded at one time. The mistake was timing. Weeding is a process that should be done gradually and continuously.[11]

The methods outlined are for your consideration. Each situation is unique. As professionals, you will be able to plan and implement the most effective weeding program for your library. The bottom line is just to take the time and do it. No matter what method you select, do not let your actions cause problems for someone else. Be considerate and be aware that your discards may be offensive to or unwanted by others.

And one final thought on the subject . . . one of the most interesting reasons given for weeding was that it burns calories. Think about the implications.

NOTES

1. Robert D. Stueart, "Weeding of Library Materials—Politics and Policies," in *Collection Management* 7 (summer 1985): 48.

2. American Association of School Librarians and Association for Educational Communications and Technology, *Information Power* (Chicago: American Library Association; Washington, D.C.: Association for Educational Communications and Technology, 1988), 73.
3. ———, *Information Power* (Chicago: American Library Association, 1998), 90.
4. Stueart, 48.
5. Phyllis J. Van Orden, *The Collection Program in Schools,* 2nd ed. (Englewood, Colo.: Libraries Unlimited, 1995), 242.
6. Ann W. Moore, "A Question of Accuracy: Errors in Children's Biographies," *School Library Journal* (February 1985): 34-35.
7. Van Orden, ibid.
8. See http//:www.sunlink.ucf.edu/weed
9. Betty Jo Buckingham, *Weeding the Library Media Center Collections* (Des Moines: State of Iowa, Department of Public Instruction, 1984), 15.
10. Ibid., 15.
11. Will Manley, "S.F.P.L. Blues," *American Libraries* (December 1996): 96.

SELECTED READINGS

Buckingham, Betty Jo. Revised by Barbara Safford. *Weeding the Library Media Center Collections.* 2nd ed. Des Moines: State of Iowa, Department of Education, 1994. http://www.iema-ia.org/IEMA209.html/ (February 2001).

Florida Department of Education School Library Media Services Office. SUNLINK Weed of the Month Club. http://www.sunlink.ucf.edu/weed/ (September 2001).

Kniffel, Leonard. "Criticism Follows Hoopla at New San Francisco Library." *American Libraries* (August 1996): 12-13.

Manley, Will. "S.F.P.L. Blues." *American Libraries* (December 1996): 96.

Manning, Pat, and Alan R. Newman. "Safety Isn't Always First: A Disturbing Look at Chemistry Books." *School Library Journal* (October 1986): 99-102.

Miller, J. Wesley. "Throwing Out Belles Lettres with the Bathwater." *American Libraries* (June 1984): 384-85.

Eloquently makes the point that librarians need to be familiar with their community and collections to avoid weeding materials that should be retained.

Moore, Ann W. "A Question of Accuracy: Errors in Children's Biographies." *School Library Journal* (February 1985): 34-35.

Identifies specific examples of errors that fall into three categories—mistakes on items (e.g., dates) that could be easily checked; errors caused by attempts to simplify content; and "patently false, incorrect information."

Stueart, Robert D. "Weeding of Library Materials—Politics and Policies." *Collection Management* (summer 1985): 47-58.

Van Orden, Phyllis. *The Collection Program in Schools: Concepts, Practices, and Information Sources.* 2nd ed. Englewood, Colo.: Libraries Unlimited, 1995.

WEBSITES FOR WEEDING

www.iema-ia.org/IEMA209.html

Weeding the Library Media Center Collections, 2nd edition, from the State of Iowa Department of Education, by Betty Jo Buckingham. Revised by Barbara Safford.

Includes the why, when, and how of weeding. Both subjective and objective weeding. Procedures. Guidelines for each Dewey class. How to discard.

www.sldirectory.com/libsf/resf/coldev2.html

General site on collection development with links to other sites; includes a section of links for weeding.

www.sunlink.ucf.edu/weed

Homepage for SUNLINK Weed of the Month Club.

www.doe.state.la.us/doe/publications/bulletins/1134/append_i.htm

Weeding guidelines from the Louisiana Department of Education.

APPENDIX A

Alternate Ways to Do Data Analysis

When we wrote our first book in 1990, many school libraries were not automated. For that reason, the original techniques for collection evaluation were devised assuming that school librarians would be working with a shelflist, card catalog, and calculator. Today, in the year 2002, automated school libraries are not uncommon. Therefore, the collection analysis techniques suggested in the main text of this book assume automated systems, computers, and spreadsheets.

At the same time, we recognize that not all school libraries are automated and not all automation systems lend themselves to doing collection evaluation. For these reasons, the original techniques based on the older systems appear in this appendix.

Sampling from a Shelflist

To use systematic random sampling (as described in chapter 2) on a traditional card shelflist, follow these steps:

1. Measure the total length of the cards in the shelflist drawers in centimeters, an easier unit to add than fractions of inches. Hold the drawers horizontally and keep the tension fairly equal from drawer to drawer. (A shelflist measuring form is suggested in figure A.1.)
2. Decide on the size of the sample. Two hundred cards is the recommended size.

3. Divide the total shelflist length (the bottom line on the shelflist measuring form) by the sample size. The quotient is the interval size. For example, if the total shelflist length is 2,680 cm, the interval is 2,680 divided by 200 or 13.4 cm.
4. Randomly select a starting point less than or equal to the interval. For example, if the interval is 13.4 cm, a number less than or equal to 134 should be selected. The final digits of dollar bill serial numbers or telephone numbers from the white pages can be used to ensure randomness. (Don't use telephone numbers you know; select unfamiliar ones from the telephone book.)
5. Beginning with the first drawer of the shelflist, measure to the starting point and insert a straight pin from the side. Then count back five cards. The first acceptable card following the fifth card is the first title in the sample. (Older card stock is heavier. Because of wear, some cards are wider at the top than others. Sampling from the side and counting back five cards helps compensate for worn cards and heavier paper, and gives all titles an equal chance of being chosen.)
6. From the starting point, measure the length of the interval to locate the second title. Measure from the second title to find the third title, and so on. If the first title is at 9.9 cm and the interval is 13.4 cm, the second title is at 9.9 plus 13.4 or 23.3 cm. The third title is at 23.3 plus 13.4 or 36.7 cm.
7. At the end of one drawer, carry over the extra centimeters to the front of the next drawer and continue measuring intervals to the end of the shelflist.

When you have reached the end of the shelflist, it is wise to count how many titles are in the sample. Often, the actual sample size will be the same as the one selected, for example, 200 titles. If there are, for example, only 197 cards, you may proceed with the collection analysis by using the number 197 instead of 200 in the calculations. Or you may randomly select a shelflist drawer, and then a location in centimeters (using phone numbers or dollar bill serial numbers) to obtain the additional titles.

In figure A.1, it is not necessary to complete every blank. Use the applicable categories and skip the others. It may be appropriate or desirable to evaluate only some kinds of materials in the collection. For example, in order to emphasize the book collection, periodicals and audiovisual materials could be omitted. Or only reference books and materials for adult readers could be surveyed. Which portion of the collection is to be evaluated depends on the purpose of the survey and the professional judgment of the librarian or media specialist.

If the library is not automated, it is easiest and most efficient to take the random sample from the shelflist. But this is not always possible. If the catalog is divided, the sample may be drawn from the title cards following the procedure given for sampling the shelflist.

Collection Percentages

Discussion of the reasons for and value of knowing collection percentages is presented in the body of this book. To calculate collection percentages based on measurement of the shelflist, use the procedure presented in figure A.2.

Average Collection Age

Another useful number is the average age of the collection, which is relatively easy to calculate from the sample cards. Use figure A.3. (It will probably be necessary to include years earlier than 1983.) Follow the steps given below:

1. In the first blank column fill in the number of titles for each year. This may be easier if the sample cards are in chronological order or are first sorted into piles.
2. For each line in the table, multiply the number of books by the year and write the product in the last column.

3. Add the products in the last column.
4. Divide this total by the number of titles in the sample. This gives the average copyright date of the sample. For example, if 1980 is the result, the average date of the collection is 1980.
5. Subtract the average copyright date from the current year to find the average age of the sample in years. For example, if the average copyright date is 1980 and the current year is 2000, the average age of the sample is twenty years old. It is also a good estimate of the average age of the collection, if the proper procedure was used to obtain the sample.

Collection Use

As stated earlier in the main body of the text, another way of evaluating the collection is by considering its use. The procedure given below will indicate circulation patterns for the collection. This information can be especially useful for weeding.

1. Sort the sample cards according to the last due date.
2. In figure A.4 fill in the first blank to show the number of titles that fall into each category.
3. Multiply the number in the first blank by 100. Then divide the result by the number of titles in the sample. Enter the result in the second blank. For example, if a sample of 200 includes 6 titles that circulated during the last month, the percent is (6 × 100) divided by 200 or 3 percent.
4. Numbers of titles or percents can be added directly in order to combine and compare titles in different parts of the collection, such as to find the percent of the collection that has not circulated in the last year.

It is possible to divide the sample into fiction and nonfiction titles and then follow the procedure given above. The data would allow comparisons to be made between circulation of fiction and nonfiction titles.

This procedure requires the last due date for all titles in the sample. Not all circulation systems keep date-due information, either in the materials or on file. If the last date due is not available, but information about circulating titles is needed, it is possible to use the circulation file. The procedure is briefly explained in the main body of this book.

Comparison to Standard Bibliographies

The main body of the text discusses the strengths and weaknesses of using standard bibliographies in collection evaluation. Use the chart and procedure given in figure A.5 to estimate the percent of the collection included in the list of recommended materials.

1. Check the sample titles against the list in the standard source.
2. Separate the sample titles into Dewey categories.
3. For each line in figure A.5 fill in the first blank (number of sample titles in that category) and the next blank (number of these titles found in the standard source).
4. Using the procedure at the bottom of figure A.5, calculate the percent of titles found in each category. For example, if a sample included 7 books of short stories, and 2 of these were in the source, the percent is (2 × 100) divided by 7 or 29 percent.
5. To calculate the overall percent of titles found in the standard source, multiply the number of titles found in the standard source by 100, and divide by the total number in the sample. For example, if a sample of 200 included 84 that were in the standard source, the percent is (84 × 100) divided by 200 or 42 percent.

Category	*Length*		
000s	____		
100s	____		
200s	____		
300s	____		
400s	____		
500s	____		
600s	____		
700s	____		
800s	____		
900s	____		
Biography	____		
		Total Nonfiction	____
Fiction	____		
Easy Books	____		
Short Stories	____		
		Total Fiction	____
Reference	____		
Audiovisual	____		
Electronic	____		
Other	____		
		Total Miscellaneous	____
		Total Shelflist	____

FIGURE A.1. Shelflist measuring form

Dewey Class	*Length in cm*	*Percent*
000s	________	________
100s	________	________
200s	________	________
300s	________	________
400s	________	________
500s	________	________
600s	________	________
700s	________	________
800s	________	________
900s	________	________
Biography	________	________
Fiction	________	________
Easy Books	________	________
Short Stories	________	________
Reference	________	________
Audiovisual	________	________

To calculate the percent for each category:

1. Multiply the number of centimeters in that category times 100.
2. Divide by the total number of centimeters in the shelflist. Use the total shelflist number from figure A.1.
3. Enter the result in the "Percent" column.

FIGURE A.2. Calculating collection percentages

Copyright Date	*Number of Books*	*Product*
2000	________	________
1999	________	________
1998	________	________
1997	________	________
1996	________	________
1995	________	________
1994	________	________
1993	________	________
1992	________	________
1991	________	________
1990	________	________
1989	________	________
1988	________	________
1987	________	________
1986	________	________
1985	________	________
1984	________	________
1983	________	________
	Total Products	________
	Number of Books in Sample	________
	Average Copyright Date	________
	Average Age of Collection	________

FIGURE A.3. Calculating average collection age

Last Due Date	*Number of Titles*	*Percent*
Less than 1 month		
1 mo – < 2 mo		
2 mo – < 3 mo		
3 mo – < 4 mo		
4 mo – < 5 mo		
5 mo – < 6 mo		
6 mo – < 1 yr		
1 yr – < 2 yr		
2 yr – < 3 yr		
3 yr – < 4 yr		
4 yr – < 5 yr		
5 yr – < 6 yr		
6 yr – < 7 yr		
7 yr – < 8 yr		
8 yr – < 9 yr		
9 yr – < 10 yr		
More than 10 yr		

1. Fill in the number of titles, which fall into each category. It is easier if you sort the index cards of the sample into piles first.
2. To calculate percent:

$$\frac{(\text{number of titles in the category}) \times 100}{\text{number of titles in the sample}}$$

3. It is possible to add number of titles or percents directly in order to combine and compare categories.
4. Feel free to adapt this form to meet the needs of your library.

FIGURE A.4. Collection use chart

Standard Source ______________________________

Dewey Class	*No. in Sample*	*No. Found in Source*	*Percent Found in Source*
000s	______	______	______
100s	______	______	______
200s	______	______	______
300s	______	______	______
400s	______	______	______
500s	______	______	______
600s	______	______	______
700s	______	______	______
800s	______	______	______
900s	______	______	______
Biography	______	______	______
Fiction	______	______	______
Easy Books	______	______	______
Short Stories	______	______	______
Reference	______	______	______
		Total Number of Titles Found	______
		Percent of Total Titles Found	______

To calculate percent:

1. Multiply by 100 the number of titles in a category found in the source (center column).
2. Divide the result by the number of sample titles in that category (first column).
3. Enter the result in the third column.

FIGURE A.5. Standard sources comparison form

APPENDIX B

Further Reading for Research and School Library Media Centers

There are articles, dissertations, and websites available that present information about how others have used data from collections to improve collection development, to communicate with others the nature of collections, or to facilitate informed management decisions. This chapter will briefly discuss selected, pertinent works that could be useful to working school library media specialists. Consult one or more of these articles if it would help you in the school library media center. It is both appropriate and prudent to learn techniques and borrow (and adapt) ideas from the published work of others. Full citations to works appear under "List of Sources," below.

General Articles and Books

If You Want to Evaluate Your Library . . . by F. W. Lancaster presents methods for evaluating almost any service in your library. While the techniques are appropriate for some very large collections, they can be readily adapted to school library media centers. The underlying research methods are sound. Five chapters deal with evaluating library collections: one each on collection quality, analysis of use, in-house use, weeding, and shelf availability.

While not specifically addressing collections, *The Tell It! Manual* by Douglas Zweizig et al., is a basic guide to the evaluation of library services. This is a good source to consult for suggested methods of gathering numbers, observing users, measuring attitudes, writing questionnaires, or interviewing students or teachers. Sound research methods are presented in plain language.

The Collection Program in Schools: Concepts, Practices, and Information Sources (Van Orden) discusses and examines all aspects of a school library media center collection. One chapter is devoted to collection evaluation and weeding is covered in another. A chart suggests ages at which certain types of materials become candidates for weeding. For example, examine history titles that are more than fifteen years old or have circulated in the last five years. This is a good reference for working school librarians because of its broad approach to the collection and extensive coverage of many related topics.

Mary Alice Anderson writes of the value of good data in running the school library media center. She uses the information she gathers on collection and circulation for budgeting, communication with administrators and teachers, and planning. For example, information about the average copyright age of the collection in graph form resulted in substantial extra funding.

Craighton Hippenhammer writes of the need for objective data to be used in managing children's library collections. He staunchly defends the time needed to gather the data and breaks the data into two categories: circulation statistics and availability statistics. This is a good source to use to defend the gathering of statistics. Hippenhammer also states that the data gathered can bring into focus areas of the collection that might be overlooked or problems that could be hidden in the surrounding forest of titles.

In the 1980s, the American Library Association and its Public Library Association worked with public libraries to develop standard means for measuring public library services. Several years later, two books were published to help standardize such statisitics for children's and young adult services: *Output Measures for Public Library Service to Children* and *Output Measures and More: Planning and Evaluating Public*

Library Services for Young Adults. These titles address such issues as in-house use of materials and fill rate (i.e., successful searches for information). These are good titles to consult for definition of some measures of library service and suggested ways to gather that information. Also, if more than one school will be involved, these titles can help to ensure that the information gathered is comparable from one school to another.

Working with Automated Systems

Many school library media centers are now automated, and the number is growing. As computers are used more and more for circulation and catalog purposes, the machines gather and create enormous amounts of data. Some articles in the literature discuss these automated systems.

Some of the automated systems are "management friendly," and the information they contain on circulation, copyright date, or holdings in the various Dewey classes or by type of material are readily available and usable. However, many of the systems are not designed so that school library media specialists are able to access and use the data stored. Kate Herzog writes of the frustrations and concerns about access to (or lack of access to) this information. Her article is a good place to start when thinking of buying or changing an automated system for the school library media center.

Age of the Collection

In Illinois, Carol Morrison and other members of the Illinois School Library Media Association's Research & Development Committee surveyed school librarians across the state. They gathered information on the number and age of titles in school libraries in three specific fields of science: astronomy, space, and the solar system; general biology and ecology; and human anatomy, physiology, and hygiene. Results are given in tables that group the data by grade levels and number of titles or grade levels and copyright dates before 1970 or copyright dates between 1990 and 1993. The results can be used for comparison with data gathered in other libraries and also show that aging collections are not a local problem only.

Carol Doll has evaluated collections in school library media centers and published in that arena. The article in *Collection Management* examines the ability of public libraries and school library media centers to support science and English curricula. Results indicate that both school and public libraries have materials to support the school curriculum. Average ages for sample titles range from nineteen to twelve years, with public library collections being generally more recent than school collections. Furthermore, there are indications that *Science Books and Films* and *Choice* are helpful for collection development in the sciences.

Doll's article in *School Library Media Quarterly* examines the concept of quality in relation to school library collections. Size of the collection, age, and comparison to the curriculum are discussed. The information on collection age might be useful for comparison in reporting your own results.

Analysis of the Use of Materials

One way to determine the value of a title is to evaluate its use in or through the media center. This has been done in several ways, as shown by the following research studies.

In her article on using circulation data for management purposes, Kathleen Garland first discusses sampling techniques. Then she uses data collected to show that, when a sample is selected correctly, the results can be generalized to the entire school year. It is not necessary to gather circulation data every day to get an accurate approximation of circulation activity. She suggests using knowledge of the collection to show support of the curriculum and to support budget requests to administrators.

Linda Bertland has worked to document ways that circulation data from automated systems can be used in managing school library media center collections. Her work demonstrates how the relationship between circulation and collection holdings can be used to inform collection development. She compares, for example, the percent of circulation for a specific Dewey classification area to the percent of the total holdings in that area. This helps to spotlight underused or overused portions of the collection. For a more complete discussion of her techniques, consult the articles in *School Library Media Quarterly.*

Chuck Hamaker examined circulation and patron statistics over time in an academic library. Most importantly, his article is an excellent example of using the information collected to help better understand collection use in the library. Hamaker makes the point that often we don't "just know" or can't guess what is happening, and good data can help with collection development. As he says, "You won't know who uses your subject area the most until you look." (p. 194)

Daniel Callison was more interested in the way students used Wilsearch/Wilsonline to locate articles pertinent to their research papers. He notes that student use of pertinent articles could be one way to identify sources the school library would need to retain or add to its holdings. Consult his article for suggestions on how to evaluate student use of databases like Wilsonline.

Related Issues

While not strictly related to collection evaluation, selection of materials in an electronic format poses unique problems for collection development. Cheryl LaGuardia and Stella Bentley present a list of questions recommended for guiding acquisition of information in CD-ROM format for university libraries. Some of these same issues are also pertinent to school library media centers.

Alternative Methods of Gathering Information

This book presents a statistically sound method that can be used by working school library media specialists to gather information about their collections in a limited amount of time. The method is based on selecting a random sample and uses a small number of titles. Using a properly selected random sample, it is possible to make some conclusions about a school library media collection without examining all of the titles available. There are other methods presented in the literature that suggest alternative ways to gather data about the collection.

In a short article, Frances Davis writes of evaluating a collection of a small community college. Faculty from each of the departments were enlisted to scrutinize holdings in their subject area and respond on the worksheet developed by the library. This article gives a quick look at their procedure, details the work the librarians did to notify the faculty and enlist their support, and includes a copy of the worksheet.

The *conspectus* is a comprehensive method that examines all of the resources available in and through a library or media center. To use such a method, first decide on the appropriate level of coverage (ranging from broad to more coverage to detailed) for a particular classification or curriculum area. Then examine the materials available in or through the collection as it now exists. Finally, use professional judgment to decide which areas of strength or weakness so identified need additional attention or resources. Janet Lange and Richard Wood present a nice overview of the conspectus and give a lengthy bibliography of references for further investigation of this technique.

David Loertscher has worked to develop a method of collection evaluation called collection mapping. In this technique, the media specialist breaks the collection into small pieces and then looks at each as needed to build, weed, or maintain that segment. The media specialist first decides which portions of the collection are basic and meet a variety of diverse needs; which portions require a general emphasis and meet demands for a whole course of instruction, such as United States history; and which portions emphasize a specific topic, such as dinosaurs. Then the total number of titles are counted and examined for each section. Decisions are made about the diversity of formats, recency, relevance, quantity, and appropriateness for the student users. Overall, this technique gives a detailed picture of the collection and involves teachers and administrators in the process. At the same time, it can be quite time-consuming.

May Lein Ho and David Loertscher further refined the collection mapping technique by investigating schools in eleven states and comparing results to national bibliographies such as *Elementary School Library Collection.* (See chapter 3 for more information about such lists.) William Murray et al. applied the technique in Aurora, Colorado, public schools, and reported that it helped school personnel take a close look at media center collections. Collection mapping is an appropriate technique for school library media center collections when an in-depth analysis is needed.

SOURCES CITED

Anderson, Mary Alice. "Data Gathering for Maximum Results." *Book Report* (January/February 1999): 16-18.

Bertland, Linda H. "Circulation Analysis as a Tool for Collection Development." *School Library Media Quarterly* 19 (winter 1991): 90-97.

———. "Usage Patterns in a Middle School Library: A Circulation Analysis." *School Library Media Quarterly* 16 (spring 1988): 200-203.

Callison, Daniel. "Methods for Measuring Student Use of Databases and Interlibrary Loan Materials." *School Library Media Quarterly* 16 (winter 1988): 138-42.

Davis, Frances. "A Plan for Evaluating a Small Library Collection." *College and Research Libraries* 54 (June 1993): 328-29.

Doll, Carol A. "Quality and Elementary School Library Media Collections." *School Library Media Quarterly* 25 (winter 1997): 95-102.

———. "School Library Media Center and Public Library Collections and the High School Curriculum." *Collection Management* 20 (1995): 99-114.

Garland, Kathleen. "Circulation Sampling as a Technique for Library Media Program Management." *School Library Media Quarterly* 20 (winter 1992): 73-78.

Hamaker, Chuck. "Time Series Circulation Data for Collection Development or: You Can't Intuit That." *Library Acquisitions: Practice and Theory* 19 (summer 1995): 191-95.

Herzog, Kate S. "Collection Development and Evaluation in the Electronic Library." In *Encyclopedia of Library and Information Science.* Vol. 53, supplement 16, 82-92. Edited by Allen Kent and Carolyn M. Hall. New York: Marcel Dekker, 1994.

Hippenhammer, Craighton. "Managing Children's Library Collections through Objective Data." *Top of the News* 42 (spring 1986): 309-13.

Ho, May Lein, and David V. Loertscher. "Collection Mapping: The Research." In *Measures of Excellence for School Library Media Centers,* ed. by David V. Loertscher, 22-39. Englewood, Colo.: Libraries Unlimited, 1988.

LaGuardia, Cheryl, and Stella Bentley. "Electronic Databases: Will Old Collection Development Policies Still Work?" *Online* 16 (July 1992): 60-63.

Lancaster, F. W. *If You Want to Evaluate Your Library. . . .* Champaign: University of Illinois Graduate School of Library and Information Science, 1988.

Lange, Janice, and Richard Wood. "The Conspectus: A Tool for Collection Assessment and Description." In *Encyclopedia of Library and Information Science.* Vol. 66, supplement 29, 65-78. Edited by Allen Kent and Carolyn M. Hall. New York: Marcel Dekker, 2000.

Loertscher, David V. "Collection Mapping: An Evaluation Strategy for Collection Development." In *Measures of Excellence for School Library Media Centers,* ed. by David V. Loertscher, 9-21. Englewood, Colo.: Libraries Unlimited, 1988.

Morrison, Carol, Carol Fox, Marti Guarin, and Kathleen Shannon. "School Library Snapshots: A Brief Survey of Illinois School Library Collections in Three Areas of Science." *Illinois Libraries* 76 (fall 1994): 211-19.

Murray, William, Marion Messervey, Barbara Dobbs, and Susan Gough. "Collection Mapping and Collection Development." In *Measures of Excellence for School Library Media Centers,* ed. by David V. Loertscher, 40-51. Englewood, Colo.: Libraries Unlimited, 1988.

Van Orden, Phyllis J., Kay Bishop, and Patricia Pawelak-Kort. *The Collection Program in Schools: Concepts, Practices, and Information Sources.* 3rd ed. Englewood, Colo.: Libraries Unlimited, 1995.

Walter, Virginia A. *Output Measures and More: Planning and Evaluating Public Library Services for Young Adults.* Chicago: American Library Association, 1995.

——— *Output Measures for Public Library Service to Children: A Manual of Standardized Procedures.* Chicago: American Library Association, 1992.

Zweizig, Douglas, Debra Wilcox Johnson, Jane Robbins, and Michele Besant. *The Tell It! Manual: The Complete Program for Evaluating Library Performance.* Chicago: American Library Association, 1996.

LIST OF SELECTED SOURCES

Date of publication and edition information are omitted in the following titles as they are updated continually.

Children's Catalog (New York: H. W. Wilson).
Elementary School Library Collection: A Guide to Books and Other Media, Phases 1-2-3, ed. L. L. Homa (Newark, N.J.: Bro-Dart). Now with accompanying CD-ROM.
Middle and Junior High School Library Catalog (New York: H. W. Wilson).
Senior High School Library Catalog (New York: H. W. Wilson).
Guide to Reference Books for School Media Centers by Christine L. Wynar (Littleton, Colo.: Libraries Unlimited).
Reference Books for Elementary and Junior High School Libraries by Carol Sue Peterson (Metuchen, N.J.: Scarecrow).
Children's Magazine Guide: Subject Index to Children's Magazines (Madison, Wisc.: Rowland).
Reader's Guide to Periodical Literature (New York: H. W. Wilson).

NATIONAL SURVEYS OF SCHOOL LIBRARY MEDIA RESOURCES

Miller, Marilyn L., and Marilyn L. Shontz. "Location Is Everything: A Region-by-Region Look at School Library Spending and Services, FY 1997-1998. *School Library Journal* 46 (November 2000): 50-60.
———. "How Do You Measure Up?" *School Library Journal* 45 (October 1999): 50-59.
———. "Plug It In: The Wired School Library." *School Library Journal* 44 (October 1998): 26-31.
———. "More Services, More Staff, More Money." *School Library Journal* 44 (May 1998): 28-33.
———. "Small Change: School Library Media Expenditures, 1995-96." *School Library Journal* 43 (October 1997): 28-37.
———. "Live Wires: High-Tech Media Specialists Get Connected." *School Library Journal* 42 (October 1996): 27-32.
———. "The Race for the School Library Dollar." *School Library Journal* 41 (October 1995): 22-33.
———. "Inside High-Tech School Library Media Centers." *School Library Journal* 40 (April 1994): 24-29.
———. "Expenditures for Resources in School Library Media Centers, FY 1991-92." *School Library Journal* 39 (October 1993): 26-36.

Carol A. Doll is a professor at the Graduate School of Library and Information Science program at Wayne State University. She is the author of numerous articles appearing in journals including *School Library Media Quarterly* and the *Journal of Youth Services in Libraries.* She is co-author of *Bibliotherapy with Young People: Librarians and Mental Health Professionals Working Together* (Libraries Unlimited, 1997) and editor of *Exploring the Pacific States through Literature* (Oryx Press, 1994). An active member of the AASL, she is currently the AASL representative to the National Committee for Accrediting Teacher Education. Doll received her doctorate from the University of Illinois.

Pamela Petrick Barron is an associate professor in the Department of Library and Information Studies at the University of North Carolina at Greensboro. She was the content and research supervisor for "Jump Over the Moon: Sharing Literature with Young Children," an award-winning, fifteen-part telecourse currently in use in the United States, Canada, Asia, and Europe. She is also the author of *Jump over the Moon: Selected Professional Readings* (Holt, 1984), *Study Guide for the Telecourse, Jump over the Moon,* and *Writers on Writing for Young Adults* (Omnigraphics, 1990). She is an active member of AASL and ALSC. Barron received her doctorate from Florida State University.